Table of Contents

Introduction	**19**
Definition Of Personal Growth And Development	20
Importance Of Personal Growth And Development	23
1. Technological Advancement	23
2. Globalization	23
3. Economic Shifts	24
4. Workplace Changes	24
5. Mental Health Awareness	24
6. Information Overload	24
7. Environmental and Social Challenges	25
Overview Of The Sub-Topics Covered In The Book	25
Mindset and Attitude	25
Self-Awareness	26
Emotional Intelligence	26
Communication Skills	27
Time Management	27
Goal Setting	28

Mindfulness	28
Stress Management	28
Personal Habits	29
Learning and Personal Development	29
Conclusion	30
1. Mindset And Attitude	**31**
The Power Of Positive Thinking	32
The Neuroscience of Positive Thinking	32
The Impact of Positive Thinking on Health	33
Practical Application	33
Cultivating A Growth Mindset	34
Thomas Edison: The Light of Persistence	34
J.K. Rowling: From Rejection to Wizardry Fame	35
Michael Jordan: A Leap from Failure to Greatness	35
Malala Yousafzai: The Power of Belief in Education	35
Overcoming Limiting Beliefs	36
Psychological Aspects of Limiting Beliefs	36
Strategies for Overcoming Limiting Beliefs	37
Practice Exercises To Improve Your Mindset	38

1. Gratitude Journaling	38
2. Growth Mindset Affirmations	39
3. Mindfulness Meditation	39
4. Best Possible Self Diary	39
5. Cognitive Restructuring	40
6. Failure Analysis Reflection	40
7. Social Comparison Reflection	40
8. Skill Development Planning	41
2. Self-Awareness	**42**
Understanding Your Values And Beliefs	43
Reflect on Key Life Moments	43
Use Established Values Inventories	44
Beliefs Questionnaires	44
Journaling Prompts	45
Mindfulness and Reflection Practices	45
Seek Feedback	45
Implementing Your Discoveries	46
Discovering Your Personality Traits	46
Personality Assessment Tools	46

The Role of Feedback in Self-Awareness	47
Engaging with Feedback	48
Understanding Your Strengths And Weaknesses	49
Identifying Strengths and Weaknesses	49
Seeking Feedback	50
Interpreting Feedback	50
Acting on Feedback	51
Practice Exercises To Increase Self-Awareness	52
1. Daily Reflection Journaling	52
2. The Five Whys Technique	52
3. Mindfulness Meditation	53
4. Role Reflection	53
5. Strengths and Weaknesses Assessment	54
6. Emotional Triggers Log	54
7. Value Clarification	54
8. Feedback Seeking and Reflection	55
3. Emotional Intelligence	**56**
Emotional Intelligence: Navigating the Landscape of Emotions	56
Self-Awareness	56

Self-Management	57
Social Awareness	57
Relationship Management	57
The Importance Of Emotional Intelligence	58
Connection to Personal Success	58
Connection to Leadership	59
Understanding And Managing Your Emotions	60
Strategies for Understanding Your Emotions	61
Exercises for Recognizing and Labeling Emotions	61
Developing Empathy And Compassion	63
1. Active Listening	64
2. Perspective-Taking	64
3. Practice Empathy in Daily Interactions	64
4. Emotional Vocabulary Expansion	65
5. Engage with Diverse Perspectives	65
6. Volunteer and Help Others	65
7. Mindfulness and Compassion Meditation	66
8. Reflect on Your Actions	66
Practice Exercises To Improve Emotional Intelligence	66

Emotional Journaling	67
Empathy-Building Activities	67
Mindfulness Meditation for Emotional Regulation	68
Gratitude Practice	69
Emotional Vocabulary Expansion	69
4. Communication Skills	**70**
The Art of Connection and Understanding	70
Key Areas Covered:	70
Understanding Effective Communication	72
Components of Effective Communication	72
The Role of Non-Verbal Communication	73
Enhancing Non-Verbal Communication	74
Improving Interpersonal Relationships	74
Case Study 1: Conflict Resolution in the Workplace	75
Case Study 2: Strengthening Family Relationships	75
Case Study 3: Building Rapport with Clients	76
Key Takeaways	77
Overcoming Communication Barriers	77
1. Language and Cultural Differences	78

2. Emotional Barriers	78
3. Physical Distractions	79
4. Technological Barriers	79
5. Psychological Barriers	80
6. Jargon and Technical Language	80
7. Listening Barriers	81
Practice Exercises To Improve Communication Skills	81
Active Listening Exercises	81
Expressive Skills Development Exercises	82
Combined Listening / Expressive Communication Exercises	83
5. Time Management	**85**
Mastering Your Moments for Maximum Impact	85
Key Areas Covered:	85
Understanding The Importance Of Time Management	87
The Pomodoro Technique	87
The Eisenhower Box	88
Strategies For Managing Time More Effectively	89
The Psychology of Procrastination	89
Strategies for Managing Time More Effectively	90

Overcoming Procrastination And Distractions	92
1. Acknowledge and Understand Your Procrastination	92
2. Break Tasks into Smaller Steps	92
3. Set Clear Goals and Deadlines	92
4. Use the Five-Minute Rule	93
5. Eliminate Distractions	93
6. Prioritize Tasks	93
7. Implement Time Management Techniques	93
8. Seek Support and Accountability	93
9. Reward Yourself	93
10. Practice Self-Compassion	94
11. Visualize Success	94
12. Adjust Your Environment	94
Practice Exercises To Improve Time Management	94
1. Time Audit	95
2. Prioritization Exercise	95
3. Goal Setting and Breaking Down	95
4. The Pomodoro Technique Trial	96
5. Weekly Planning Session	96

6. Time Blocking Method	97
7. Daily Reflection and Adjustment	97
6. Goal Setting	**98**
Charting Your Path to Success	98
Key Areas Covered:	98
The Benefits Of Goal Setting	99
Benefits of Goal Setting	100
SMART Goals and Beyond	101
Setting Meaningful And Achievable Goals	102
Understand Your Why	102
Set Goals Aligned with Your Values	102
Break Down Big Goals	103
Embrace SMART Criteria	103
Regularly Review and Adjust Goals	103
Visualize Success	104
Build Accountability	104
Staying Motivated And On Track	104
1. Set Clear, Achievable Goals	105
2. Break Down Goals into Smaller Tasks	105

3. Create a Visual Representation of Your Goals	105
4. Find Your Why	105
5. Use Positive Affirmations	105
6. Implement a Reward System	106
7. Maintain a Support System	106
8. Track and Celebrate Progress	106
9. Adjust Goals as Needed	106
10. Engage in Regular Self-Reflection	106
11. Limit Distractions	106
12. Practice Self-Compassion	107
13. Visualize Success	107
Practice Exercises To Improve Goal Setting Skills	107
Exercise 1: Define Your Vision and Set Long-Term Goals	107
Exercise 2: Create a Goal-Mapping Template	108
Exercise 3: Develop a Progress Tracking Template	108
Exercise 4: Set and Review Weekly Goals	109
Exercise 5: Reflective Journaling	109
7. Mindfulness	**111**
The Path to Presence and Clarity	111

Key Areas Covered:	111
Understanding Mindfulness And Its Benefits	113
The Science Behind Mindfulness	113
Integrating Mindfulness	115
Integrating Mindfulness Into Daily Life	115
1. Mindful Breathing	116
2. Mindful Eating	116
3. Mindful Walking	116
4. Body Scan Meditation	116
5. Mindful Listening	116
6. Pause and Observe	117
Resources for Further Practice	117
The Benefits Of Mindfulness Meditation	118
Benefits of Mindfulness Meditation	118
Variety of Mindfulness Meditation Techniques	119
Practice Exercises To Improve Mindfulness	121
1. Mindful Morning Routine	121
2. Mindful Breathing Breaks	121
3. Mindful Observation	122

4. Mindful Listening	122
5. Mindful Eating	122
6. Mindful Walking	123
7. Gratitude Reflection	123
8. Body Scan Meditation	123
8. Stress Management	**125**
Navigating Life's Pressures with Grace and Resilience	125
Key Areas Covered:	125
Understanding The Impact Of Stress	127
The Impact of Stress	127
Identifying Personal Stress Triggers	128
Strategies for Managing Stress	129
Techniques For Reducing Stress	130
1. Aromatherapy	131
2. Art Therapy	131
3. Forest Bathing (Shinrin-yoku)	131
4. Laughter Yoga	131
5. Biofeedback	132
6. EFT Tapping (Emotional Freedom Techniques)	132

7. Tai Chi or Qigong	132
8. Sound Therapy	133
9. Guided Imagery	133
10. Journaling for Gratitude	133
Improving Resilience And Coping Skills	134
1. Self-Assessment	134
2. Recognize Your Stressors	134
3. Build on Your Strengths	134
4. Develop a Toolkit of Coping Strategies	135
5. Practice Mindfulness and Emotional Regulation	135
6. Set Realistic Goals	135
7. Cultivate a Positive Outlook	135
8. Foster Social Connections	136
9. Learn from Experience	136
10. Seek Professional Help When Needed	136
Practice Exercises For Stress Management	137
1. Keeping a Stress Diary	137
2. Deep Breathing Exercises	137
3. Progressive Muscle Relaxation (PMR)	138

4. Mindfulness Meditation	138
5. Guided Imagery	139
6. Physical Activity	139
9. Personal Habits	**140**
Personal Habits: The Building Blocks of a Fulfilling Life	140
Key Areas Covered:	140
Understanding The Role Of Habits	142
Keystone Habits: A Foundation for Change	142
Characteristics of Keystone Habits	142
Examples of Keystone Habits	143
Developing Keystone Habits	144
Developing Healthy Habits	144
Developing Healthy Habits	144
Habit-Tracking Template	146
Digital Tools Recommendations	147
Breaking Negative Habits	148
1. Understand Your Habits	148
2. Set Clear, Achievable Goals	148
3. Find a Substitute Behavior	148

4. Change Your Environment	149
5. Use Reminders and Cues for Positive Habits	149
6. Implement a Tracking System	149
7. Seek Support	149
8. Reward Yourself	149
9. Practice Self-Compassion	150
10. Be Patient and Persistent	150
11. Consider Professional Help	150
Practice Exercises To Improve Personal Habits	150
1. Identify and Understand Your Current Habits	151
2. Set Clear, Specific Goals	151
3. Implement the Replacement Technique	151
4. Develop Mini Habits	151
5. Use Habit Stacking	151
6. Create a Supportive Environment	152
7. Employ Visual Cues and Reminders	152
8. Track Your Progress	152
9. Reward Yourself for Milestones	152
10. Reflect and Adjust	153

10. Learning And Personal Development — **154**

- Lifelong Journeys of Growth — 154
- Key Areas Covered: — 154
- Importance Of Continuous Learning — 156
- Adaptability Through Continuous Learning — 156
- Resilience Through Personal Development — 157
- Practical Benefits of Personal Development — 157
- Strategies for Incorporating Personal Development — 158
- Strategies For Continuous Learning And Growth — 159
- The Role of Mentorship — 159
- Strategies for Effective Mentorship — 160
- The Importance of Networking — 160
- Strategies for Effective Networking — 161
- Reading, Attending Courses, And Pursuing Experiences — 162
- Reading Resources — 162
- Online Course Platforms — 163
- Experiential Learning Opportunities — 163
- Practice Exercises To Improve Personal Development Skills — 164
- 1. Create a Personalized Learning Plan — 164

2. Engage in Reflective Practice	165
3. Seek Feedback	166
4. Set Up a Peer Learning Group	167
Conclusion	**168**
Conclusion: Embracing the Journey of Personal Growth	168
Key Takeaways:	168
Recap Of The Main Points Covered In The Book	170
1. Introduction to Personal Growth and Development	170
2. Mindset and Attitude	170
3. Self-Awareness	170
4. Emotional Intelligence	170
5. Communication Skills	171
6. Time Management	171
7. Goal Setting	171
8. Mindfulness	171
9. Stress Management	171
10. Personal Habits	171
11. Learning and Personal Development	172
Conclusion	172

Final Thoughts On Personal Growth And Development	172
Call to Action	173
Encouragement To Continue The Journey	175
Encouragement for Your Journey	175
Resources for Continued Learning and Development	175

Introduction

In a world that moves at an ever-accelerating pace, the journey towards personal growth and development has never been more essential. "Personal Development" is designed as a comprehensive guide to help you navigate the multifaceted landscape of self-improvement. This book is not just a collection of theories but a practical roadmap to enriching your life through deliberate actions and mindset shifts.

At the heart of personal development lies the belief that everyone possesses the innate potential to transform their lives. Whether you seek to enhance your emotional intelligence, improve your communication skills, manage stress more effectively, or cultivate a growth mindset, this book offers the tools and insights necessary for personal and professional advancement.

Through a combination of research-backed strategies, real-life anecdotes, and practical exercises, "Personal Development" aims to guide you on a journey of self-discovery and growth. Each chapter is dedicated to a key aspect of personal development, from understanding and managing your emotions to setting meaningful goals and developing resilience against life's challenges.

As you embark on this journey, you'll find that personal growth is not a destination but a continuous process of learning, adapting, and evolving. This book invites you to challenge limiting beliefs, embrace change, and unlock your potential. With each page, you'll be encouraged to reflect, act, and transform your mindset and habits to lead a more fulfilling and purposeful life.

"Personal Development" is more than just a book; it's a companion on your journey towards becoming the best version of yourself. Let's embark on this transformative journey together, equipped with the knowledge, skills, and determination to make lasting changes. Welcome to the first step of a journey that promises growth, learning, and an ever-expanding horizon of possibilities.

Definition Of Personal Growth And Development

Personal growth and development is a lifelong process of self-improvement that involves expanding one's knowledge, skills, and understanding to achieve one's full potential. It encompasses a wide range of activities and practices aimed at enhancing one's abilities, quality of life, and realizing personal goals and aspirations. This process is deeply personal and can vary significantly from one individual to another, reflecting each person's unique ambitions, values, and circumstances.

At its core, personal growth and development involve cultivating a deeper sense of self-awareness. This means understanding one's strengths and weaknesses, values, beliefs, and motivations. It's about identifying personal objectives and working towards them, whether they relate to professional success, improved relationships, spiritual enlightenment, or emotional well-being.

Key components of personal growth and development include:

Self-awareness: Gaining insights into oneself, including one's passions, talents, and areas for improvement.

Learning and knowledge acquisition: Continuously seeking new information, skills, and experiences to expand one's understanding and competencies.

Emotional intelligence: Developing the ability to recognize, understand, and manage one's own emotions and those of others to enhance personal and professional relationships.

Resilience and adaptability: Cultivating the ability to bounce back from setbacks and adapt to changing circumstances with flexibility and strength.

Goal setting and achievement: Setting clear, achievable goals and developing strategies and plans to reach them.

Habit formation: Identifying and cultivating habits that support one's goals and personal well-being while working to eliminate those that do not.

Health and wellness: Maintaining physical health through exercise, proper nutrition, and self-care practices, as well as mental health through stress management and mindfulness.

Personal growth and development are not static; they require ongoing effort, reflection, and adjustment as one's needs and circumstances evolve. This process is fundamentally about moving towards a more fulfilling, effective, and authentic life, enabling individuals to not only achieve their personal and professional goals but also contribute positively to the world around them.

Personal growth and development refer to the process of improving oneself through such activities as enhancing self-awareness, acquiring new knowledge, developing talents and potential, building human capital, and facilitating employability. It encompasses the cultivation of personal qualities, the pursuit of personal and professional goals, and the deepening of relationships with oneself and others. This holistic process involves not just the mind but also the emotions, physical health, social connections, and spiritual understanding.

A real-life example that illustrates the transformative power of personal growth and development is the story of Chris Gardner. Gardner's journey from homelessness to becoming a successful stockbroker, businessman, and motivational speaker is a testament to the power of resilience, determination, and self-improvement. Despite facing severe financial instability and the responsibility of caring for his young son as a single parent, Gardner never lost sight of his aspirations. He invested in his personal growth by learning the ins and outs of the financial industry, often studying and preparing for his broker's license after long hours of work and caring for his son. His commitment to personal development, amidst seemingly insurmountable challenges, eventually led to a position at a prestigious brokerage firm, laying the groundwork for his future success.

Another example is J.K. Rowling, who, before becoming one of the world's most successful authors, faced numerous rejections and personal challenges, including living as a single mother on welfare. Rowling's journey of writing the "Harry Potter" series while navigating personal hardships demonstrates the importance of perseverance, self-belief, and the continuous pursuit of one's passion and goals. Her story underscores the transformative potential of embracing one's creative talents and persisting in the face of adversity.

These examples underscore that personal growth and development are not merely about achieving success in a conventional sense but about overcoming obstacles, discovering and leveraging one's strengths, and continuously striving for a better, more fulfilled life. Through the process of personal development, individuals can transform their lives, impact those around them, and contribute to a broader societal good.

Importance Of Personal Growth And Development

In today's rapidly evolving world, personal growth and development have become more than just concepts of self-improvement; they are essential tools for navigating the complexities and uncertainties of modern life. The importance of personal development is magnified by several key dynamics that characterize the contemporary landscape:

1. Technological Advancement

The swift pace of technological innovation has transformed how we work, communicate, and live. While technology offers vast opportunities, it also demands continuous learning and adaptation. Personal growth equips individuals with the agility to adapt to new tools and platforms, ensuring they remain relevant and competitive in their personal and professional lives.

2. Globalization

The world has become increasingly interconnected, bringing diverse cultures, ideas, and challenges into closer contact. Personal development fosters cultural awareness and empathy, enabling individuals to navigate and thrive in a globalized environment by understanding and appreciating different perspectives and adapting to varied social contexts.

3. Economic Shifts

Economic landscapes are shifting, with traditional career paths becoming less linear and the gig economy rising. Personal development helps individuals cultivate a mindset of resilience, creativity, and entrepreneurship, essential for navigating economic uncertainties and capitalizing on emerging opportunities.

4. Workplace Changes

The nature of work is evolving, with an emphasis on soft skills such as emotional intelligence, adaptability, and collaborative ability. Investing in personal growth allows individuals to develop these competencies, enhancing their effectiveness in the workplace and their ability to lead, innovate, and work within teams.

5. Mental Health Awareness

As awareness of mental health issues grows, so does the recognition of practices like mindfulness, stress management, and emotional regulation as critical components of personal well-being. Personal development activities can support mental health by providing strategies to manage stress, build resilience, and cultivate a positive mindset.

6. Information Overload

The digital age has brought an unprecedented volume of information, which can be overwhelming. Personal growth and development teach critical thinking, discernment, and the ability to focus on what truly matters, helping individuals make informed decisions and maintain clarity in a cluttered information landscape.

7. Environmental and Social Challenges

The modern world faces significant environmental and social challenges, from climate change to social inequality. Personal development encourages a sense of responsibility and empowerment, inspiring individuals to contribute positively to their communities and the planet.

Personal growth and development, therefore, are not merely about self-fulfillment; they are critical for adapting to and thriving in the modern world. By cultivating a commitment to lifelong learning, resilience, and adaptability, individuals can navigate the complexities of today's global landscape, seize opportunities, and face challenges with confidence and purpose. This process enables not only personal success and satisfaction but also a meaningful contribution to the broader societal good.

Overview Of The Sub-Topics Covered In The Book

"Personal Development" is crafted to guide readers through a holistic journey of self-improvement, touching on various dimensions of personal and professional growth. The book is structured to offer a comprehensive exploration of key areas essential for development, each designed to build upon the other, creating a cohesive and transformative experience. Here is an overview of the sub-topics covered, highlighting the range of topics and the practical, actionable advice provided:

Mindset and Attitude

Fostering Positive Thinking: Techniques to cultivate an optimistic outlook and reframe challenges.

Cultivating a Growth Mindset: Strategies to embrace learning and view failures as opportunities for growth.

Overcoming Limiting Beliefs: Identifying and dismantling the mental barriers that hinder progress.

Practice Exercises: Real-world applications to strengthen mental resilience and adaptability.

Self-Awareness

Values and Beliefs Exploration: Exercises to clarify personal values and align actions with beliefs.

Personality and Strengths Discovery: Tools to understand innate traits and leverage them effectively.

Acknowledging Weaknesses: Strategies for addressing and mitigating personal limitations.

Practice Exercises: Activities designed to enhance self-knowledge and authenticity.

Emotional Intelligence

Importance and Development: Understanding the role of emotional intelligence in personal and professional success.

Managing Emotions: Techniques for regulating emotions and responding to the emotions of others.

Empathy and Compassion: Cultivating understanding and connection with others.

Practice Exercises: Practical steps to improve emotional awareness and interpersonal relationships.

Communication Skills

Effective Communication Fundamentals: Principles of clear and empathetic communication.

Interpersonal Relationship Enhancement: Strategies to build and maintain strong relationships.

Overcoming Barriers: Identifying and addressing common communication obstacles.

Practice Exercises: Exercises to develop active listening, assertiveness, and feedback skills.

Time Management

Understanding Time's Value: Approaches to prioritize tasks and maximize productivity.

Effective Strategies: Techniques for efficient time use, including goal setting and scheduling.

Dealing with Procrastination: Methods to overcome procrastination and maintain focus.

Practice Exercises: Tools and templates to implement effective time management practices.

Goal Setting

Benefits and Techniques: Setting SMART goals and other frameworks to achieve personal and professional objectives.

Motivation Maintenance: Keeping motivated through setbacks and progress plateaus.

Monitoring Progress: Methods for tracking advancements and adjusting goals as needed.

Practice Exercises: Goal-setting worksheets and action plans to realize ambitions.

Mindfulness

Mindfulness and Its Benefits: Introduction to mindfulness practices and their impact on well-being.

Daily Integration: Strategies to incorporate mindfulness into everyday life.

Mindfulness Meditation: Guided practices for beginners and advanced practitioners.

Practice Exercises: Exercises to cultivate presence, awareness, and calm in daily activities.

Stress Management

Understanding Stress: Identifying stressors and their effects on health and productivity.

Reduction Techniques: Coping mechanisms and strategies to manage and reduce stress.

Building Resilience: Strengthening emotional and mental fortitude to handle future stressors.

Practice Exercises: Relaxation techniques and resilience-building activities.

Personal Habits

Habit Formation and Change: Understanding the psychology behind habit development.

Healthy Habit Cultivation: Strategies for creating and maintaining beneficial habits.

Breaking Negative Habits: Techniques for identifying and overcoming destructive patterns.

Practice Exercises: Habit trackers and challenge plans to support habit transformation

Learning and Personal Development

Continuous Learning Importance: Emphasizing lifelong learning as a pillar of personal growth.

Learning Strategies: Approaches to absorb new knowledge and skills effectively.

Seeking Experiences: Encouraging experiential learning and personal expansion.

Practice Exercises: Plans and prompts to foster a learning mindset and practical application.

Conclusion

Recap of Key Insights: Summarizing the essential lessons and strategies shared throughout the book.

Encouragement for Ongoing Growth: Motivating readers to continue their personal development journey beyond the book.

Each chapter not only delves into the theoretical aspects of its topic but also provides readers with actionable advice, exercises, and tools to apply the concepts in their daily lives. "Personal Development" serves as both a comprehensive guide to understanding the facets of personal growth and a practical companion to effect real, lasting change.

1. Mindset And Attitude

Embarking on a journey of personal growth and development, the foundation upon which all progress is built, is our mindset and attitude. These are the lenses through which we view the world, interpret challenges, and perceive opportunities. They shape our thoughts, influence our emotions, and drive our actions. This section of the book is dedicated to exploring the profound impact that our mindset and attitude can have on our lives, both personally and professionally.

A positive mindset and a growth-oriented attitude are not just beneficial; they are essential for anyone looking to improve themselves and achieve their goals. These elements empower us to overcome obstacles, learn from failures, and continuously strive for excellence. We will delve into the power of positive thinking, demonstrating how a shift in perspective can transform challenges into stepping stones towards success. Through cultivating a growth mindset, we learn to embrace the process of learning and view setbacks not as insurmountable barriers but as opportunities for development and growth.

Moreover, this section addresses the common hindrance of limiting beliefs—those deeply ingrained convictions that constrain our potential and stifle our progress. We will explore strategies to identify, challenge, and overcome these barriers, thereby unlocking our true capabilities.

To ensure that these concepts are not just theoretical but also practical and actionable, we will introduce a series of practice exercises designed to enhance your mindset and attitude. These exercises are crafted to foster resilience, adaptability, and a proactive approach to life's challenges and opportunities.

By the end of this section, you will have gained invaluable insights into the power of your mindset and attitude, equipped with the tools to cultivate a perspective that supports your journey towards personal and professional fulfillment. Whether you are looking to achieve career success, improve your relationships, or simply live a more contented life, the principles and practices outlined here will serve as your guide to transforming your internal dialogue and, by extension, your external reality.

The Power Of Positive Thinking

The power of positive thinking is more than just a motivational phrase; it's a principle backed by neuroscience, revealing how our thoughts can shape our reality, influence our health, and impact our overall success in life. Positive thinking isn't about ignoring life's problems; instead, it involves approaching unpleasantness in a more positive and productive way, believing that the best is yet to come.

The Neuroscience of Positive Thinking

Research in neuroscience has shown that positive thinking activates regions of the brain associated with reduced anxiety and improved mental health. One key area is the prefrontal cortex, which is involved in planning complex cognitive behavior, personality expression, decision-making, and moderating social behavior. Positive thoughts can stimulate growth in this region, enhancing our ability to think more clearly and solve problems more effectively.

Another aspect of neuroscience research focuses on the neuroplasticity of the brain, which is its ability to form new neural connections throughout life. Positive thinking and optimistic attitudes can strengthen neural pathways that promote feelings of well-being and resilience. This means that through the practice of positive thinking, we can rewire our brains to be more inclined towards positivity, improving our mental health and emotional resilience over time.

The Impact of Positive Thinking on Health

Positive thinking has been linked to a wide range of health benefits, including longer life span, lower rates of depression, lower levels of distress, greater resistance to the common cold, better psychological and physical well-being, better cardiovascular health and reduced risk of death from cardiovascular disease, and better coping skills during hardships and times of stress.

One mechanism behind these benefits is that positive thinking may reduce the harmful effects of stress on the body. When we think positively, our body's stress response is diminished, which can lead to improved health outcomes. Moreover, a positive outlook enables individuals to adopt healthier lifestyles, as they are more likely to exercise, eat well, and avoid harmful behaviors.

Practical Application

Incorporating positive thinking into daily life involves recognizing negative thought patterns and consciously choosing to focus on positive aspects and outcomes. Techniques such as gratitude journaling, mindfulness meditation, and cognitive-behavioral strategies can help individuals cultivate a more positive mindset. These practices not only improve mental health but can also lead to better decision-making, enhanced creativity, and improved interpersonal relationships.

The transformative power of positive thinking, underpinned by neuroscience, offers a compelling argument for adopting an optimistic outlook. By understanding and leveraging the brain's capacity for change, we can foster a mindset that not only enhances our well-being but also propels us toward achieving our fullest potential.

Cultivating A Growth Mindset

Cultivating a growth mindset, a concept popularized by psychologist Carol Dweck, involves believing that one's talents and abilities can be developed through dedication and hard work. This perspective contrasts with a fixed mindset, where individuals see their qualities as static and unchangeable. Embracing a growth mindset unlocks potential, fosters resilience, and encourages a love for learning and a willingness to confront challenges. Below, we feature stories of individuals who have overcome limiting beliefs through adopting a growth mindset, illustrating its transformative power.

Thomas Edison: The Light of Persistence

Thomas Edison, one of the most prolific inventors in history, embodies the essence of a growth mindset. Edison faced numerous failures and setbacks in his quest to invent a practical electric light bulb. Legend has it that he experienced over a thousand unsuccessful attempts before finally succeeding. Rather than viewing these failures as a sign of incapacity, Edison famously regarded them as steps towards success, stating, "I have not failed. I've just found 10,000 ways that won't work." Edison's perseverance and willingness to learn from each setback highlight the core of a growth mindset: seeing failure not as a barrier but as a vital part of the learning process.

J.K. Rowling: From Rejection to Wizardry Fame

J.K. Rowling's journey to becoming the author of the Harry Potter series is another powerful testament to the growth mindset. Rowling faced rejection from twelve publishing houses before "Harry Potter and the Philosopher's Stone" was finally accepted. During this period, she battled personal challenges, including the loss of her mother, divorce, and financial difficulties while raising her daughter as a single parent. Rowling's persistence, belief in her potential, and openness to feedback and improvement reflect a growth mindset. Her story exemplifies how embracing challenges and persevering in the face of adversity can lead to unprecedented success.

Michael Jordan: A Leap from Failure to Greatness

Michael Jordan, considered one of the greatest basketball players of all time, was cut from his high school basketball team because his coach thought he lacked skill. Instead of giving up, Jordan used this rejection as motivation to work harder, practicing tirelessly to improve his game. His dedication paid off, leading to an illustrious career with six NBA championships and numerous accolades. Jordan's ability to use failure as a catalyst for growth and his relentless pursuit of excellence are hallmarks of a growth mindset.

Malala Yousafzai: The Power of Belief in Education

Malala Yousafzai, a Pakistani activist for female education and the youngest Nobel Prize laureate, faced life-threatening challenges in advocating for her beliefs. After surviving an assassination attempt by the Taliban, Malala could have retreated in fear. Instead, she continued to fight for education rights with even greater resolve. Her recovery and return to activism demonstrate a growth mindset, showing that even the most severe setbacks can be overcome with resilience and a commitment to personal development.

These stories illuminate the essence of a growth mindset: the belief that through effort, perseverance, and learning from failure, individuals can exceed their limitations and achieve remarkable accomplishments. By cultivating a growth mindset, we can all learn to embrace challenges, persist in the face of setbacks, and view failure not as evidence of unintelligence but as a heartening springboard for growth and for stretching our existing abilities.

Overcoming Limiting Beliefs

Limiting beliefs are deeply held convictions that constrain our potential, shaping our perception of ourselves and the world around us. These beliefs often stem from past experiences, societal messages, or the influence of significant figures in our lives. They can manifest in various aspects of our lives, from our professional ambitions to our personal relationships, and can significantly hinder our growth and happiness. Understanding the psychological underpinnings of these beliefs and employing strategies to overcome them is essential for personal development.

Psychological Aspects of Limiting Beliefs

Cognitive Biases: Limiting beliefs are often reinforced by cognitive biases such as confirmation bias, where we seek out information that confirms our pre-existing beliefs and ignore evidence to the contrary.

Self-Fulfilling Prophecies: These beliefs can lead to self-fulfilling prophecies, where our expectations influence our actions in such a way that we bring about what we anticipate.

Fear of Failure: Many limiting beliefs are rooted in a fear of failure or rejection. This fear can paralyze us, preventing us from taking risks or trying new things.

Identity and Self-Concept: Limiting beliefs are tightly woven into our self-concept. They shape how we see ourselves and what we believe we are capable of achieving.

Strategies for Overcoming Limiting Beliefs

Awareness and Identification: The first step in overcoming limiting beliefs is to become aware of them. This involves self-reflection and honesty about the narratives we tell ourselves. Journaling, mindfulness practices, and therapy can aid in identifying these beliefs.

Challenge and Question: Once identified, challenge these beliefs by asking critical questions: Is this belief true? What evidence do I have to support or refute this belief? Are there instances where this belief has not held true?

Reframe Your Thoughts: Cognitive-behavioral strategies can help reframe limiting beliefs into more positive, empowering beliefs. For example, instead of thinking, "I'm not good at public speaking," reframe it to, "I can improve my public speaking skills with practice and preparation."

Set Small, Achievable Goals: Setting and achieving small goals can help build confidence and dismantle limiting beliefs. Each success provides evidence against the limiting belief and strengthens new, more positive beliefs.

Seek Support: Friends, mentors, or professionals who can provide perspective and feedback can be invaluable. They can help you see when you're being influenced by a limiting belief and encourage you to challenge it.

Visualization and Positive Affirmations: Visualizing success and using positive affirmations can help reprogram your subconscious mind, replacing limiting beliefs with empowering ones.

Learning and Growth Mindset: Embrace a growth mindset, where you view challenges as opportunities to learn and grow. This perspective shifts focus from fearing failure to valuing the growth that comes from trying, regardless of the outcome.

Expose Yourself to New Experiences: New experiences can challenge our limiting beliefs by proving we're capable of more than we thought. This could be as simple as learning a new skill or as significant as traveling solo.

By understanding the psychological roots of our limiting beliefs and actively employing strategies to overcome them, we can unlock our potential and open ourselves up to new possibilities and opportunities. Overcoming limiting beliefs is not a one-time event but a continuous process of growth and self-discovery.

Practice Exercises To Improve Your Mindset

Improving your mindset is a transformative process that involves both understanding the science behind mindset shifts and engaging in practical exercises that promote growth and positivity. The following practice exercises, grounded in research and incorporating elements of personal reflection, are designed to help you cultivate a more positive, resilient, and growth-oriented mindset.

1. Gratitude Journaling

Research Basis: Studies have shown that gratitude journaling can significantly increase well-being and life satisfaction.

Exercise: Every day, write down three things you are grateful for. These can be as simple as a sunny day or as significant as the support of a loved one. The practice encourages you to focus on the positive aspects of your life, shifting your mindset from what you lack to what you have.

2. Growth Mindset Affirmations

Research Basis: Positive affirmations can rewire the brain to adopt a more growth-oriented mindset by reinforcing beliefs in one's ability to grow and improve.

Exercise: Create a list of growth mindset affirmations, such as "I am capable of learning and growing," or "Challenges help me grow." Repeat these affirmations to yourself each morning or whenever you face a challenge.

3. Mindfulness Meditation

Research Basis: Mindfulness meditation has been linked to reduced stress, improved focus, and a shift towards positive thinking.

Exercise: Dedicate a few minutes each day to mindfulness meditation. Focus on your breath and observe your thoughts and feelings without judgment. This practice helps develop a present-centered mindset, reducing negative rumination.

4. Best Possible Self Diary

Research Basis: Visualizing your best possible self can boost your mood, increase optimism, and enhance your belief in your abilities.

Exercise: Spend some time writing about your life in the future where everything has gone as well as it possibly could. Describe what you have achieved and how you did it. This exercise encourages you to focus on your potential and the steps needed to reach your goals.

5. Cognitive Restructuring

Research Basis: Cognitive restructuring, a core component of cognitive-behavioral therapy, helps identify and challenge negative thought patterns.

Exercise: When you catch yourself engaging in negative self-talk or harboring limiting beliefs, write down the thought, then challenge it. Ask yourself evidence-based questions to dispute the negative or limiting belief and replace it with a more balanced or positive thought.

6. Failure Analysis Reflection

Research Basis: Reflecting on failures and analyzing them constructively can foster resilience and a growth mindset by highlighting opportunities for learning and improvement.

Exercise: Think about a recent failure or setback. Write down what happened, how it made you feel, what you learned from it, and how you can apply these lessons in the future. This exercise transforms failure from a negative outcome to a valuable learning experience.

7. Social Comparison Reflection

Research Basis: Reflecting on how social comparisons affect your mindset can help reduce their negative impact and foster self-compassion.

Exercise: Whenever you find yourself comparing your achievements or lifestyle to others', write down your thoughts and feelings. Then, shift your focus to your own journey and progress, acknowledging your unique path and successes.

8. Skill Development Planning

Research Basis: Setting goals for skill development and achieving them can enhance self-efficacy and a growth mindset.

Exercise: Identify a skill you'd like to improve or learn. Break down the learning process into small, manageable steps and set a timeline for achieving them. Celebrate your progress along the way, reinforcing your belief in your ability to grow and improve.

Incorporating these exercises into your daily or weekly routines can help you gradually shift your mindset towards one that embraces growth, positivity, and resilience. Remember, changing your mindset is a journey that requires patience, practice, and persistence.

2. Self-Awareness

At the heart of personal growth lies the foundational pillar of self-awareness. This critical aspect of personal development involves delving deep into the essence of who we are: understanding our thoughts, emotions, values, and the driving forces behind our actions. Self-awareness is the starting point from which meaningful change can emanate, enabling us to navigate life's complexities with greater clarity, purpose, and fulfillment.

Embarking on the journey toward heightened self-awareness invites us to explore the multifaceted dimensions of our being. It challenges us to confront our deepest values and beliefs, recognize

our unique personality traits, and acknowledge both our strengths and our weaknesses. This exploration is not always comfortable, but it is invariably enriching, offering invaluable insights that pave the way for authentic living and well-being.

In this section of the book, we delve into the critical components of self-awareness and provide practical strategies to cultivate it. Through understanding your values and beliefs, you can align your actions with what truly matters to you, leading to a more meaningful and satisfying life. Discovering your personality traits allows you to leverage your natural tendencies and adapt in areas where you may face challenges. Recognizing your strengths and weaknesses empowers you to capitalize on your assets and address areas for improvement, setting the stage for personal and professional growth.

Moreover, we offer practice exercises designed to enhance self-awareness. These exercises are not just reflective but are also rooted in the latest psychological research, ensuring they are both effective and transformative. From guided self-reflection to targeted activities that reveal deeper layers of your psyche, these practices are tailored to help you embark on a journey of discovery and insight.

Embracing self-awareness is an act of courage. It requires an openness to self-examination and a willingness to grow. As you navigate through this section, remember that the journey to self-awareness is ongoing—a perpetual unfolding of understanding that enriches every aspect of your life. With each step forward, you unlock new potentials for growth, leading to a more authentic, empowered, and fulfilling life.

Understanding Your Values And Beliefs

Understanding your values and beliefs is a fundamental step in the journey towards self-awareness and personal development. Values are the guiding principles that shape our behavior and decision-making processes, while beliefs are the convictions we hold to be true. Together, they form the foundation of our identity, influencing our choices, goals, and interactions with the world around us. To gain deeper insights into your values and beliefs, self-assessment tools and quizzes can be invaluable resources. Here's how you can start this process of exploration and understanding:

Reflect on Key Life Moments

Begin by reflecting on moments in your life that felt particularly fulfilling or meaningful. Ask yourself:

What was happening?
Who were you with?
What values were you honoring in these moments?

This reflection can help pinpoint values that are truly significant to you.

Use Established Values Inventories

Several well-researched values inventories can guide you in identifying your core values. Some popular ones include:

The Values in Action (VIA) Survey: Focuses on identifying character strengths and virtues.

The Schwartz Value Survey: Categorizes values into ten broad values such as achievement, benevolence, tradition, and power.

The Personal Values Assessment (PVA) by Barrett Values Centre: Helps you to identify what is most important to you and how these values guide your actions.

These inventories often provide detailed results that explain how your values influence various aspects of your life.

Beliefs Questionnaires

Beliefs are often shaped by our experiences, culture, and upbringing. To understand your beliefs, consider questionnaires that explore:

Core Beliefs Inventory: This type of inventory can help you uncover fundamental beliefs about yourself, others, and the world—beliefs that influence your perception and behavior.

Limiting Beliefs Questionnaires: These are designed to help you identify beliefs that may be holding you back from achieving your full potential.

Journaling Prompts

Journaling can be a powerful tool for exploring your values and beliefs. Some prompts to get you started might include:

What values do you believe are most important in maintaining a good society?

Think about a time you were angry or upset. What value or belief was challenged?

Describe a belief you hold about success, failure, love, or happiness. Where do you think this belief came from?

Mindfulness and Reflection Practices

Mindfulness can heighten self-awareness, allowing you to observe your thoughts and reactions without judgment. Through regular mindfulness practice, you might begin to notice patterns in your thoughts and behaviors that reflect underlying values and beliefs.

Seek Feedback

Sometimes, others can offer valuable insights into our values and beliefs. Ask trusted friends, family members, or colleagues about what values they see you demonstrating in your life. This external perspective can provide a new angle from which to understand yourself.

Implementing Your Discoveries

Understanding your values and beliefs is not just an exercise in self-knowledge—it's about bringing that understanding into your daily life. Once you have a clearer picture of your values and beliefs,

consider how they align with your current lifestyle, career, and relationships. This alignment is crucial for living authentically and making decisions that bring you fulfillment and happiness.

By engaging with these self-assessment tools and reflective practices, you embark on a meaningful exploration of your inner landscape. This journey not only fosters a deeper sense of self-awareness but also equips you with the knowledge to live a life that truly reflects who you are at your core.

Discovering Your Personality Traits

Discovering your personality traits is a crucial aspect of self-awareness that can significantly impact your personal and professional life. Understanding your personality helps in navigating social interactions, choosing career paths, and managing stress and conflicts. Personality assessment tools and the role of feedback from others are two valuable methods for gaining insights into your personality traits.

Personality Assessment Tools

Several scientifically validated tools can help you discover your personality traits. These assessments offer structured frameworks to understand the various dimensions of personality:

The Myers-Briggs Type Indicator (MBTI): One of the most popular personality tools, the MBTI, categorizes individuals into 16 personality types based on four dichotomies: Introversion/Extraversion, Sensing/Intuition, Thinking/Feeling, and Judging/Perceiving. This tool helps individuals understand their preferences in processing information, making decisions, and interacting with the world.

The Big Five Personality Traits: Also known as the Five-Factor Model, it evaluates personality across five broad dimensions: Openness, Conscientiousness, Extraversion, Agreeableness, and Neuroticism (OCEAN). This model is widely used in psychological research to predict behavior and psychological well-being.

The Enneagram: A model of human psyche which is principally understood and taught as a typology of nine interconnected personality types. This tool is useful for self-discovery, personal growth, and understanding relationship dynamics.

The Role of Feedback in Self-Awareness

While self-assessment tools provide a structured approach to understanding your personality, feedback from others offers invaluable insights that can deepen self-awareness. Here's how feedback plays a critical role:

Mirror to Blind Spots: Feedback can reveal blind spots in our self-perception, highlighting aspects of our personality that we may not be aware of. It acts as a mirror, reflecting how our behaviors and traits are perceived by others.

Validation of Self-Assessment: It can validate or challenge our self-assessment, offering an external perspective that complements our self-understanding. This can confirm traits we believe we have or reveal discrepancies between how we see ourselves and how others perceive us.

Enhancing Personal Growth: Constructive feedback provides a basis for personal development. Understanding how certain traits affect our interactions and relationships can motivate us to develop skills such as empathy, communication, and emotional intelligence.

Navigating Social Relationships: Feedback helps us understand the impact of our personality traits on social interactions. By being aware of how others perceive our behaviors, we can adapt and improve our social skills, enhancing both personal and professional relationships.

Engaging with Feedback

To make the most of feedback, it's important to seek it proactively and from a variety of sources, including friends, family, colleagues, and supervisors. Approach feedback with an open mind and a willingness to learn. Consider the following steps:

Ask Specific Questions: Instead of asking for general feedback, ask specific questions about behaviors or situations to gain more actionable insights.

Reflect on Feedback: Take time to reflect on the feedback received. Consider how it aligns with your self-perception and what changes, if any, you might want to make.

Develop an Action Plan: Based on the feedback and your reflections, develop an action plan to address areas for improvement. Set specific, achievable goals for personal growth.

Discovering your personality traits through self-assessment tools and feedback is a dynamic process that evolves over time. By continuously engaging in self-discovery and being receptive to feedback, you can enhance your self-awareness, leading to more informed decisions, better relationships, and a more fulfilling life.

Understanding Your Strengths And Weaknesses

Understanding your strengths and weaknesses is a pivotal aspect of self-awareness that fosters personal and professional growth. Recognizing what you excel at allows you to leverage your strengths, while being aware of your weaknesses can guide you towards areas for improvement and development. Seeking and interpreting feedback effectively is crucial in this process, as it provides objective insights into your abilities and behaviors. Here's how you can navigate this journey:

Identifying Strengths and Weaknesses

Self-Reflection: Begin with introspection. Consider situations where you've felt most successful or satisfied. What skills were you using? Conversely, think about moments of challenge or failure. What difficulties did you encounter?

Personality and Skill Assessments: Utilize tools like the StrengthsFinder, Myers-Briggs Type Indicator (MBTI), or the Big Five Personality Test to gain insights into your inherent strengths and potential areas for development.

Journaling: Keep a journal of daily successes and challenges. Over time, patterns will emerge that highlight your strengths and weaknesses.

Seeking Feedback

Choose the Right People: Seek feedback from a diverse group of people who know you in different capacities—colleagues, supervisors, friends, and family. Ensure they are individuals who can provide honest, constructive feedback.

Be Specific in Your Request: Rather than asking for general feedback, ask specific questions. For instance, inquire about how you handle teamwork, manage stress, or contribute to projects. This specificity makes it easier for others to provide useful insights.

Create a Safe Environment: Let people know that you value their feedback and that it's safe for them to be honest with you. Emphasize that you're seeking feedback to grow and improve.

Interpreting Feedback

Listen Actively: When receiving feedback, listen attentively without interrupting. Ask clarifying questions if necessary. This demonstrates respect for the feedback giver and ensures you fully understand their perspective.

Seek Examples: When feedback is given, ask for specific examples to better understand the context and your behavior in those situations.

Separate Emotion from Information: It's natural to have an emotional response to feedback, especially if it's about areas for improvement. Try to view feedback as valuable information for growth, not as personal criticism.

Look for Patterns: If multiple sources highlight similar strengths or weaknesses, these areas are likely accurate reflections of your abilities and behaviors.

Acting on Feedback

Reflect on the Feedback: Take time to process the feedback. Reflect on how it aligns or conflicts with your self-perception.

Develop an Action Plan: For identified strengths, consider how you can further leverage them in your personal and professional life. For weaknesses, create a plan for development, which might include training, mentoring, or practice.

Follow Up: After you've worked on your areas for improvement, seek feedback again to assess your progress. This shows your commitment to growth and allows you to adjust your action plan as needed.

Understanding your strengths and weaknesses through self-assessment and feedback is a dynamic process that requires openness, humility, and a commitment to continuous improvement. By effectively seeking and interpreting feedback, you can gain valuable insights that propel your personal and professional development.

Practice Exercises To Increase Self-Awareness

Increasing self-awareness is a foundational step in personal growth, allowing you to understand your behaviors, emotions, motivations, and their impact on your life and others. Engaging in specific exercises can deepen this understanding, leading to more informed choices and actions. Here are practice exercises that include both guided self-reflection and assessment activities designed to enhance your self-awareness:

1. Daily Reflection Journaling

Exercise: Dedicate time each day to write in a journal. Focus on three key questions:

What did I do today?
What feelings did I experience, and why?
What did I learn about myself?

Purpose: This practice encourages you to reflect on daily experiences, identify patterns in your behavior and emotions, and recognize learning opportunities.

2. The Five Whys Technique

Exercise: When you encounter a problem or a strong emotional reaction, ask yourself "why" five times to drill down to the underlying cause.

Example: If you're upset about receiving feedback, ask "Why am I upset?" and continue asking "why" to each answer to delve deeper into your feelings and beliefs.

Purpose: This technique helps uncover root causes of your reactions, shedding light on your underlying beliefs and values.

3. Mindfulness Meditation

Exercise: Practice mindfulness meditation for a few minutes each day, focusing on your breath and observing your thoughts and feelings without judgment.

Guidance: Use guided meditation apps or videos if you're a beginner to help you stay focused and learn the technique.

Purpose: Mindfulness increases your awareness of the present moment, helping you become more aware of your thoughts and feelings and their transient nature.

4. Role Reflection

Exercise: Write down the various roles you play in your life (e.g., parent, friend, employee). For each role, reflect on the following:

What are my responsibilities in this role?
What values am I expressing through this role?
How do I feel about my performance in this role?

Purpose: This exercise helps you understand how different aspects of your identity influence your behavior and self-perception.

5. Strengths and Weaknesses Assessment

Exercise: Make a two-column list of your perceived strengths and weaknesses. Next, seek feedback from friends, family, or colleagues to compare perceptions.

Follow-up: Reflect on any discrepancies or surprises in the feedback and consider how this new understanding might impact your self-perception.

Purpose: This activity enhances self-awareness by comparing your self-assessment with external perceptions, providing a more rounded view of yourself.

6. Emotional Triggers Log

Exercise: Keep a log of instances when you experienced strong emotions. Note the trigger, your reaction, and the outcome.

Analysis: After a week, review the log to identify patterns in what triggers your emotions and how you respond.

Purpose: Understanding your emotional triggers and reactions promotes emotional intelligence and self-regulation.

7. Value Clarification

Exercise: List your top five values and provide examples of how you live these values in your daily life. Consider any discrepancies between your values and actions.

Reflection: Reflect on any misalignments and how you might better align your actions with your values.

Purpose: This exercise helps you clarify what truly matters to you and assess how well your life reflects your values.

8. Feedback Seeking and Reflection

Exercise: Actively seek feedback on a specific aspect of your behavior or work. Ask for specific examples and suggestions for improvement.

Integration: Reflect on the feedback, considering how it aligns with your self-perception and what changes you might make based on this input.

Purpose: Regularly seeking and reflecting on feedback promotes a growth mindset and continuous self-improvement.

Incorporating these exercises into your routine can significantly enhance your self-awareness, providing a foundation for personal growth, improved relationships, and greater fulfillment in life.

3. Emotional Intelligence

Emotional Intelligence: Navigating the Landscape of Emotions

In the realm of personal development, emotional intelligence stands as a pivotal cornerstone, shaping our ability to understand, use, and manage emotions in positive ways. This critical skill set enables individuals to communicate effectively, empathize with others, overcome challenges, and defuse conflict, facilitating both personal and professional success. At its core, emotional intelligence involves four key components: self-awareness, self-management, social awareness, and relationship management.

This section of the book delves into the intricate world of emotional intelligence, offering insights and strategies to enhance your capacity in each of these areas. By fostering a deep understanding of your own emotions, you can better navigate your emotional landscape, leading to improved decision-making and stress management. Simultaneously, enhancing your ability to perceive and understand the emotions of others paves the way for more meaningful and productive relationships.

Self-Awareness

We begin by exploring self-awareness, the foundation of emotional intelligence, which involves recognizing and understanding your own emotions and how they affect your thoughts and behavior. This awareness is crucial for personal growth, as it influences how we perceive ourselves and our interactions with the world around us.

Self-Management

Following self-awareness, we delve into self-management, focusing on the skills necessary to regulate and control our emotional

responses. Mastering this aspect of emotional intelligence allows for greater adaptability and resilience, enabling us to navigate life's ups and downs with grace and poise.

Social Awareness

Social awareness, or the ability to understand the emotions and needs of others, is next. This component emphasizes empathy and active listening, key skills for building rapport and fostering strong relationships. Through social awareness, we learn to navigate social complexities with sensitivity and kindness.

Relationship Management

Finally, we address relationship management, which brings together the previous components to manage interactions successfully. This section offers strategies for effective communication, conflict resolution, and how to inspire and influence others positively.

Throughout this exploration of emotional intelligence, we provide practical exercises and real-life examples to cultivate these skills. From enhancing self-awareness through reflection and mindfulness to developing empathy and relationship management strategies, this guide offers a comprehensive toolkit for anyone looking to thrive in the emotionally complex world we navigate daily.

Embracing and enhancing your emotional intelligence is not merely a journey of personal enrichment but a pathway to a more empathetic, understanding, and connected world. Let us embark on this transformative journey together, unlocking the full potential of our emotional intelligence to lead more fulfilling and harmonious lives.

The Importance Of Emotional Intelligence

Emotional intelligence (EI) has emerged as a critical factor for achieving personal success and effective leadership. Unlike traditional measures of intelligence (IQ), which focus on analytical and problem-solving abilities, emotional intelligence encompasses the ability to recognize, understand, manage, and use emotions in positive ways to relieve stress, communicate effectively, empathize with others, overcome challenges, and defuse conflict. The importance of emotional intelligence in both personal success and leadership roles cannot be overstated, as it directly influences how we manage our behavior, navigate social complexities, and make personal decisions that achieve positive results.

Connection to Personal Success

Self-awareness and Self-regulation: Individuals with high emotional intelligence are more aware of their emotional states and are better equipped to regulate them. This self-awareness and self-regulation contribute to greater mental health, job performance, and well-being. By understanding and managing their emotions, individuals can make more rational decisions, maintain stability under pressure, and cope with life's challenges more effectively.

Motivation: Emotional intelligence is closely linked to personal motivation. Those with high EI are more adept at self-motivation, setting and achieving goals, and maintaining a positive outlook in the face of setbacks. Their intrinsic motivation helps them pursue goals with energy and persistence, directly contributing to personal and professional success.

Empathy and Relationships: A key component of emotional intelligence is empathy, the ability to understand and share the feelings of others. Empathetic individuals are better at building and

maintaining strong personal and professional relationships, an essential aspect of personal success. Good relationships are not only critical for happiness and well-being but also for networking, collaboration, and support in both personal and professional contexts.

Connection to Leadership

Influence and Social Skills: Leaders with high emotional intelligence can influence their teams more effectively. They use their emotional awareness and social skills to inspire and motivate others, foster respect and loyalty, and create a positive, productive work environment. Effective leaders use their EI to navigate social networks, build alliances, and understand the emotional currents within their organization.

Conflict Resolution: Emotional intelligence plays a crucial role in conflict resolution. Leaders with high EI are skilled at identifying the underlying emotions and perspectives involved in a conflict, allowing them to mediate effectively and find solutions that address the concerns of all parties involved. This ability to manage and resolve conflict is essential for maintaining team cohesion and productivity.

Adaptability and Change Management: The ability to manage emotions and remain calm and clear-headed under stress is a hallmark of emotionally intelligent leaders. This adaptability is particularly important in today's fast-paced and ever-changing business environment. Leaders who can manage their emotions and the emotions of others during times of change can help guide their teams through uncertainty, fostering resilience and a positive attitude towards change.

Developing Others: A leader with high emotional intelligence can recognize the strengths and weaknesses of their team members and provide feedback and development opportunities tailored to each individual. By understanding and addressing the emotional and developmental needs of their team, emotionally intelligent leaders can cultivate talent, encourage growth, and build a strong, capable team.

In conclusion, emotional intelligence is a powerful predictor of personal success and effective leadership. By fostering emotional intelligence, individuals can enhance their own well-being and achieve their personal and professional goals, while leaders can create more cohesive, motivated, and high-performing teams. The development of emotional intelligence skills is therefore not just beneficial but essential for anyone looking to succeed in today's complex social and professional landscapes.

Understanding And Managing Your Emotions

Understanding and managing your emotions is a crucial aspect of emotional intelligence that impacts your decision-making, relationships, and overall well-being. The ability to recognize and label your emotions accurately is the first step towards managing them effectively. Here are strategies and exercises designed to enhance your ability to understand and regulate your emotions:

Strategies for Understanding Your Emotions

Emotional Awareness: Cultivate an awareness of your emotional state by regularly checking in with yourself throughout the day. Ask yourself, "What am I feeling right now?" and "Why might I be feeling this way?"

Keep an Emotion Journal: Documenting your emotions and the circumstances in which they occur can help you identify patterns in your emotional responses and triggers.

Mindfulness Meditation: Practice mindfulness meditation to enhance your awareness of the present moment, including your feelings and thoughts. Mindfulness can help you observe your emotions without judgment, allowing you to understand them more deeply.

Exercises for Recognizing and Labeling Emotions

The Body Scan:

Purpose: To connect physical sensations with emotional states.

Exercise: Sit or lie down in a comfortable position. Close your eyes and take a few deep breaths. Starting from the top of your head and moving down to your toes, notice any physical sensations in your body. Identify areas of tension, discomfort, or relaxation. Reflect on the emotions associated with these sensations. This exercise helps link physical states to emotions, aiding in their recognition.

The Emotion Wheel:

Purpose: To improve emotional granularity by using precise labels for feelings.

Exercise: Use an emotion wheel, a tool that categorizes emotions from basic to more nuanced feelings. Start by identifying a primary emotion you're experiencing (e.g., happy, sad, angry) and then use the wheel to find more specific descriptors (e.g., content, melancholy, frustrated). This practice encourages the use of precise language to describe your feelings, enhancing emotional understanding.

Three-Step Emotional Check-In:

Purpose: To practice recognizing and accepting emotions.

Exercise: Several times a day, pause for a brief emotional check-in:

Identify: Name the emotion you're feeling.

Understand: Consider what might have triggered this emotion.

Accept: Allow yourself to feel the emotion without judgment or immediate reaction. Acknowledge that emotions are transient and informative.

Reflection Through Art or Writing:

Purpose: To explore and express emotions creatively.

Exercise: When experiencing strong emotions, engage in a creative activity such as drawing, painting, or writing. Try to express your feelings through your chosen medium. Afterward, reflect on the experience and the emotions expressed. This can provide insights into your feelings and serve as a therapeutic outlet.

The "Why" Technique:

Purpose: To uncover deeper emotions and their origins.

Exercise: When you identify an emotion, ask yourself "Why do I feel this way?" Continue to ask "why" at least four more times to dig deeper into the root cause of the emotion. This technique can reveal underlying belefs or circumstances influencing your emotional state.

Developing a nuanced understanding of your emotions and the ability to manage them is a lifelong journey. By regularly practicing these exercises, you can enhance your emotional intelligence, leading to improved self-regulation, decision-making, and relationship management.

Developing Empathy And Compassion

Empathy and compassion are essential components of emotional intelligence that enrich our connections with others, fostering understanding, support, and deep, meaningful relationships.

Empathy, the ability to understand and share the feelings of another, and compassion, the desire to help those who are suffering, both require practice and intentionality to develop fully. Here are strategies to enhance your capacity for empathy and compassion:

1. Active Listening

Strategy: Practice active listening by giving your full attention to the speaker, acknowledging their feelings, and responding appropriately without judgment.

Application: In conversations, focus on the speaker's words, tone, and body language. Nod in acknowledgment, paraphrase what has been said to show understanding, and ask open-ended questions to encourage deeper sharing.

2. Perspective-Taking

Strategy: Consciously attempt to see situations from the perspective of others. This involves imagining yourself in someone else's situation, understanding their thoughts and feelings.

Application: When someone is experiencing difficulty, try to imagine what they are going through. Reflect on questions like, "How would I feel in this situation?" or "What could be going through their mind right now?"

3. Practice Empathy in Daily Interactions

Strategy: Use everyday interactions as opportunities to practice empathy. This could be with friends, family, colleagues, or even strangers.

Application: Engage with people around you with the intent to understand their experiences and emotions. This could be as simple as acknowledging the cashier at a store or having a meaningful conversation with a coworker.

4. Emotional Vocabulary Expansion

Strategy: Enhance your emotional vocabulary to better identify and understand feelings, both your own and others'.

Application: Learn new emotion words and practice using them to describe feelings. This can help in accurately understanding and conveying emotions, facilitating deeper empathy.

5. Engage with Diverse Perspectives

Strategy: Expose yourself to stories, cultures, and experiences different from your own. This can broaden your understanding of the human experience and foster empathy.

Application: Read books, watch films, or attend cultural events that offer insights into the lives of people from different backgrounds. Reflect on their perspectives and how their experiences shape their feelings and actions.

6. Volunteer and Help Others

Strategy: Volunteering and helping others can naturally develop compassion and empathy, as it puts you in direct contact with those in need.

Application: Participate in community service activities or volunteer for causes that aid people. Focus on understanding the challenges faced by those you're helping and reflect on how you can make a positive difference in their lives.

7. Mindfulness and Compassion Meditation

Strategy: Practice mindfulness and compassion meditation to cultivate a compassionate and empathetic mindset.

Application: Engage in daily meditation practices that focus on developing loving-kindness and compassion. For example, the "Metta" meditation involves silently repeating phrases like "May you be happy. May you be free from suffering." first for yourself, then for loved ones, acquaintances, and even those you have difficulties with.

8. Reflect on Your Actions

Strategy: Regularly reflect on your interactions and behaviors, assessing how empathetic or compassionate you were and identifying areas for improvement.

Application: Keep a journal where you reflect on daily interactions, noting moments where you felt you successfully connected with someone's emotions, as well as times you might have fallen short. Consider what you could do differently in the future.

Developing empathy and compassion is a journey that not only enhances your relationships but also contributes to a more understanding and caring world. By integrating these strategies into your daily life, you can strengthen your emotional connections with others and foster a deeper sense of community and belonging.

Practice Exercises To Improve Emotional Intelligence

Improving emotional intelligence (EI) involves enhancing your ability to understand, use, and manage your own emotions in positive ways to relieve stress, communicate effectively, empathize with others, overcome challenges, and defuse conflict. Here are several practice exercises, including emotional journaling and empathy-building activities, designed to boost your EI:

Emotional Journaling

Purpose: To enhance self-awareness of your emotions and the situations that trigger them.

Exercise: Keep a daily journal where you record your emotional experiences. For each significant emotion you feel, note the following:

1. The context or situation in which the emotion occurred.
2. The specific emotion felt and its intensity.
3. Your immediate reaction or how you expressed this emotion.

Any subsequent thoughts or reflections about the situation and your emotional response.

Reflection: At the end of each week, review your entries to identify patterns in your emotional responses and triggers. Reflect on how you managed your emotions and consider alternative strategies for responding in the future.

Empathy-Building Activities

Purpose: To cultivate empathy by actively trying to understand and share the feelings of others.

Active Listening Exercise:

Activity: Engage in a conversation where your primary goal is to understand the other person's perspective fully. Use active listening techniques such as nodding, summarizing what the speaker said, and asking open-ended questions to delve deeper.

Reflection: After the conversation, reflect on how well you understood the speaker's emotions and perspective. Consider how this understanding affected your response to them.

Role Reversal:

Activity: In a situation of conflict or misunderstanding, try to see the issue from the other person's point of view. Actively imagine yourself in their position, considering their emotions and the reasons behind their actions.

Reflection: Reflect on how this perspective-taking affected your feelings about the situation. Did it change your response or approach to resolving the conflict?

Mindfulness Meditation for Emotional Regulation

Purpose: To improve your ability to regulate and manage your emotions.

Exercise: Practice mindfulness meditation regularly, focusing on your breath and observing your thoughts and emotions without judgment. When you notice an emotion, acknowledge it, name it, and then gently return your focus to your breath.

Reflection: After meditation, reflect on any emotions that arose. Consider what might have triggered these emotions and how acknowledging and observing them without immediate reaction can help you manage them more effectively.

Gratitude Practice

Purpose: To shift focus from negative to positive emotions and enhance overall emotional well-being.

Exercise: Each day, write down three things you are grateful for. Try to be specific and include a variety of aspects of your life, from personal achievements to simple pleasures.

Reflection: Reflect on how this practice affects your mood and outlook over time. Notice if it leads to an increase in positive emotions and a more optimistic perspective.

Emotional Vocabulary Expansion

Purpose: To improve emotional awareness and expression by expanding your emotional vocabulary.

Exercise: Create a list of emotion words and aim to learn new ones regularly. Challenge yourself to use these new words in your journaling and daily conversations to more accurately express your feelings.

Reflection: Reflect on how expanding your emotional vocabulary helps you better understand and articulate your emotions and those of others.

By incorporating these exercises into your routine, you can significantly enhance your emotional intelligence, leading to improved interpersonal relationships, better stress management, and a deeper understanding of yourself and those around you.

4. Communication Skills

The Art of Connection and Understanding

In the tapestry of human interaction, communication skills are the threads that bind us, enabling us to share ideas, express feelings, and forge connections. Mastering the art of communication is essential for personal and professional success, as it encompasses not only the words we choose but also how we convey and interpret messages through tone, body language, and listening. Effective communication fosters understanding, resolves conflicts, builds trust, and enhances relationships, making it a cornerstone of emotional intelligence.

This section of the book is dedicated to unraveling the complexities of communication, offering insights and strategies to enhance your ability to communicate effectively. We explore the multifaceted nature of communication, including verbal, non-verbal, and written forms, and provide guidance on how to adapt your communication style to various situations and audiences.

Key Areas Covered:

Understanding Effective Communication: We begin by defining what constitutes effective communication and the barriers that can hinder it. Understanding these foundational elements sets the stage for improving how we express ourselves and interpret others.

Active Listening: The essence of communication is not just in speaking but in listening. We delve into the art of active listening—fully concentrating, understanding, responding, and then remembering what is being said—highlighting its role in fostering empathy and deepening connections.

Non-Verbal Communication: Beyond words, our body language, facial expressions, and tone of voice convey powerful messages. We explore how to read and use non-verbal cues to enhance the clarity and emotional depth of our interactions.

Assertiveness and Emotional Honesty: Communicating your needs and feelings clearly and respectfully, without aggression, is vital. We discuss strategies for assertive communication that respects both your rights and those of others.

Conflict Resolution: Misunderstandings and disagreements are inevitable. We provide techniques for navigating conflicts constructively, focusing on problem-solving and maintaining positive relationships even in challenging conversations.

Empathy in Communication: Understanding and sharing the feelings of others can transform interactions. We examine how to cultivate empathy and integrate it into your communication style, enabling more compassionate and effective exchanges.

Adapting Communication in Digital Contexts: In our increasingly digital world, the rules of engagement can shift. We cover best practices for clear, respectful, and effective communication in emails, social media, and other digital platforms.

Throughout this section, we offer practical exercises and real-life examples to apply these principles, enhancing your communication skills in personal relationships, the workplace, and beyond. Whether you're seeking to improve your interpersonal relationships, achieve professional success, or simply express yourself more clearly and confidently, mastering the art of communication is a journey well worth undertaking. Let us guide you through the nuances of effective communication, opening doors to deeper understanding and connection in every aspect of your life.

Understanding Effective Communication

Effective communication is a multifaceted skill crucial for building relationships, resolving conflicts, and fostering understanding and collaboration in both personal and professional contexts. It involves not only the clear articulation of thoughts and ideas but also active listening, empathy, and the ability to adapt one's communication style to the audience and situation. A significant component of effective communication, often underestimated, is non-verbal communication, which can complement, reinforce, or even contradict what is said verbally.

Components of Effective Communication

Clear Messaging: Conveying your ideas and thoughts in a clear, concise manner, avoiding ambiguity and ensuring your message is understood as intended.

Active Listening: Engaging fully with the speaker, understanding their message, responding appropriately, and remembering what was said. It's about listening to understand, not just to reply.

Empathy and Understanding: Putting yourself in the other person's shoes to better understand their perspective, which can greatly enhance the effectiveness of your communication.

Feedback: Providing and receiving feedback constructively to affirm understanding and to continue improving communication skills.

Adaptability: Adjusting your communication style based on the context, situation, and audience to ensure your message is received well.

The Role of Non-Verbal Communication

Non-verbal communication includes facial expressions, body language, gestures, eye contact, posture, and tone of voice. It plays a crucial role in conveying emotions and attitudes, often providing cues that are more honest than verbal communication. Understanding and effectively using non-verbal signals can significantly enhance the quality of your interactions.

Facial Expressions: The human face is extremely expressive, able to convey countless emotions without saying a word. Matching your facial expressions with your words increases the sincerity and effectiveness of your communication.

Gestures: Deliberate movements and signals, like nodding, pointing, or waving, can help articulate and reinforce your messages.

Posture and Body Orientation: The way you stand or sit, how you position your arms and legs, and your proximity to others can convey interest, openness, aggression, or indifference.

Eye Contact: Maintaining appropriate eye contact signals confidence, attentiveness, and respect for the speaker. It plays a key role in engaging the audience and fostering a connection.

Tone of Voice: The tone, pitch, loudness, and pace of your voice can communicate emotional nuances and emphasis, affecting how your message is perceived.

Enhancing Non-Verbal Communication

Awareness: Be conscious of your non-verbal cues and how they might be interpreted. Ensure they align with your verbal messages.

Observation: Pay attention to others' non-verbal signals to better understand their feelings and reactions. This can guide how you respond verbally.

Practice: Work on controlling your non-verbal expressions to more accurately reflect your intentions and emotions. This can involve practicing in front of a mirror or recording yourself to observe your non-verbal cues.

Feedback: Seek feedback from trusted individuals about your non-verbal communication to identify areas for improvement.

Understanding and mastering both verbal and non-verbal aspects of communication can dramatically improve your ability to connect and engage with others, navigate social situations, and achieve desired outcomes in personal and professional settings. By aligning verbal messages with positive non-verbal cues, you enhance trust, clarity, and rapport, making your communication truly effective.

Improving Interpersonal Relationships

Improving interpersonal relationships through effective communication is fundamental to personal and professional success. Effective communication fosters understanding, trust, and respect, which are the pillars of strong relationships. Here, we explore how effective communication strategies have been applied in various contexts through illustrative case studies, highlighting the transformative power of these approaches.

Case Study 1: Conflict Resolution in the Workplace

Background: In a mid-sized tech company, a project team faced recurring conflicts between two key members, Alex and Jordan, due to misunderstandings and miscommunications about project roles and responsibilities. Tensions escalated, impacting team morale and productivity.

Intervention: The team leader, recognizing the need for intervention, arranged a mediation session. The session began with each party expressing their perspective using "I" statements to avoid placing blame, a technique to ensure the conversation remained focused on feelings and perceptions rather than accusations.

Outcome: Through active listening and empathetic responses, Alex and Jordan realized the root of their conflict was a lack of clear communication and misunderstanding of each other's strengths and workload capacities. They agreed on a more transparent way of assigning tasks and regular check-ins to ensure alignment. Over time, the team's productivity and morale improved significantly, demonstrating the effectiveness of open, empathetic communication in resolving workplace conflicts.

Case Study 2: Strengthening Family Relationships

Background: Maria and her teenage daughter, Elena, experienced growing tensions at home, primarily due to miscommunications and assumptions about each other's actions and intentions. The situation led to frequent arguments and emotional distance.

Intervention: Seeking to rebuild their relationship, Maria initiated a weekly "family meeting" where each could share feelings, concerns, and needs without interruption. They used reflective listening, a technique where the listener repeats back what they've heard to confirm understanding, to ensure both felt heard and understood.

Outcome: These meetings helped Maria and Elena appreciate each other's perspectives and work through misunderstandings. Over time, their relationship grew stronger, characterized by mutual respect and improved communication. This case illustrates how dedicated time for open dialogue and active listening can repair and strengthen family bonds.

Case Study 3: Building Rapport with Clients

Background: Sam, a financial advisor, struggled to retain clients and receive referrals, which he attributed to a highly competitive market. However, upon reflection, he realized the issue might be his communication approach, which was more transactional than relational.

Intervention: Sam decided to change his approach by focusing more on understanding his clients' personal and financial goals, fears, and values. He employed empathetic listening and asked open-ended questions to encourage clients to share more about their lives beyond finances.

Outcome: By demonstrating genuine interest and empathy, Sam built stronger rapport with his clients, who began to see him not just as an advisor but as a trusted confidant. Client satisfaction and retention rates improved, and referrals increased. This case underscores the importance of empathy and personal connection in building client relationships.

Key Takeaways

These case studies highlight several key strategies for improving interpersonal relationships through effective communication:

Use of "I" Statements and Active Listening: Helps keep conversations non-confrontational and ensures all parties feel heard and understood.

Reflective Listening: Validates the speaker's feelings and promotes deeper understanding.

Empathy and Open-Ended Questions: Encourage sharing and build rapport, showing genuine interest in the other person's perspective.

Effective communication is a skill that can transform relationships, resolve conflicts, and build stronger connections, as demonstrated by these case studies By practicing these strategies, individuals can enhance their interpersonal relationships across various contexts.

Overcoming Communication Barriers

Overcoming communication barriers is essential for effective interaction in both personal and professional settings. These barriers can stem from a variety of sources including linguistic differences, cultural misunderstandings, emotional distress, physical distractions, or even technological glitches. Recognizing and addressing these barriers is the first step toward improving communication. Here are several common barriers and practical solutions to overcome them:

1. Language and Cultural Differences

Barrier: Misinterpretations arising from linguistic nuances or cultural norms can lead to misunderstandings.

Solutions:

Use Clear and Simple Language: Avoid jargon, slang, and idiomatic expressions that may not be understood by speakers of other languages.

Be Culturally Sensitive: Educate yourself about the cultural backgrounds of your communication partners. Respect cultural norms and practices in your communication.

Seek Clarification: When in doubt, ask for clarification to ensure understanding.

2. Emotional Barriers

Barrier: Strong emotions like anger, sadness, or anxiety can hinder the ability to listen and communicate effectively.

Solutions:

Practice Emotional Regulation: Techniques such as deep breathing, mindfulness, or taking a short break can help manage emotions before engaging in communication.

Empathize: Try to understand the emotional state of the other person and acknowledge their feelings. This can help de-escalate emotions and facilitate clearer communication.

3. Physical Distractions

Barrier: Environmental noise, poor internet connections, or uncomfortable meeting spaces can distract from the message being communicated.

Solutions:

Choose an Appropriate Setting: Conduct conversations in quiet, comfortable environments to minimize distractions.

Ensure Good Technological Setup: For virtual communications, use reliable technology and test your setup beforehand to prevent interruptions.

4. Technological Barriers

Barrier: Over reliance on electronic communication can lead to misinterpretations and a lack of personal connection.

Solutions:

Mix Communication Methods: Use a combination of communication methods (e.g., face-to-face, phone, email) depending on the message's complexity and emotional content.

Provide Context: When using text-based communication, provide sufficient context to prevent misunderstandings. Consider using emoticons or explicit expressions of tone (e.g., "I'm saying this with a smile") sparingly and appropriately to add clarity.

5. Psychological Barriers

Barrier: Prejudices, stereotypes, or previous experiences can lead to biased communication or assumptions.

Solutions:

Keep an Open Mind: Approach conversations without preconceived notions. Focus on listening actively and understanding the other

 person's perspective.

Address Biases: Acknowledge and work on personal biases that may affect how you interpret messages from others.

6. Jargon and Technical Language

Barrier: Using industry-specific jargon or technical language can exclude or confuse those not familiar with the terminology.

Solutions:

Adapt Your Language: Tailor your language to the audience's level of understanding. When technical terms are necessary, provide clear explanations.

Use Visuals: Diagrams, charts, and illustrations can help convey complex information more clearly than verbal descriptions alone.

7. Listening Barriers

Barrier: Not truly listening to the speaker, but rather waiting for a chance to speak, can lead to misunderstandings and missed information.

Solutions:

Practice Active Listening: Show that you are listening through verbal affirmations and non-verbal cues like nodding. Summarize what the speaker has said to confirm understanding before responding.

Overcoming communication barriers requires effort, awareness, and adaptability. By employing these practical solutions, individuals can enhance their communication effectiveness, leading to more productive and fulfilling interactions.

Practice Exercises To Improve Communication Skills

Improving communication skills, particularly in areas of active listening and expressive abilities, is essential for effective interpersonal interactions. The following exercises are designed to enhance your listening and speaking skills, facilitating clearer and more meaningful communication.

Active Listening Exercises

The Paraphrase Challenge

Objective: To practice understanding and reflecting the speaker's message.

Activity: Pair up with a partner and have them share a story or opinion. After they speak, paraphrase their message to show understanding. The speaker then provides feedback on the accuracy and completeness of your paraphrase.

Non-Verbal Cue Awareness

Objective: To enhance awareness of non-verbal communication cues.

Activity: In conversations, pay close attention to the speaker's body language, facial expressions, and tone of voice. After the conversation, jot down the non-verbal cues observed and how they complemented or contradicted the verbal message.

Active Listening Role Play

Objective: To develop active listening skills in different scenarios.

Activity: Engage in role-playing exercises where each person adopts a specific role in a given scenario (e.g., customer service complaint, family disagreement). Practice active listening by acknowledging feelings, asking open-ended questions, and summarizing the speaker's points.

Expressive Skills Development Exercises

Storytelling Sessions

Objective: To improve verbal expression and storytelling skills.

Activity: Organize storytelling sessions with friends or colleagues where each person shares a personal story. Focus on clarity, pacing, and emotional expression. Receive feedback on your storytelling elements, including engagement and delivery.

Elevator Pitch Practice

Objective: To enhance concise and persuasive communication.

Activity: Develop a short "elevator pitch" about yourself, a project, or an idea. Practice delivering it to different audiences, focusing on clarity, enthusiasm, and persuasiveness. Seek feedback on the effectiveness of your message and delivery.

Expressive Writing

Objective: To cultivate the ability to express thoughts and feelings clearly in writing.

Activity: Engage in daily expressive writing exercises, such as journaling about your day, emotions, or a particular topic. Focus on conveying your thoughts and feelings clearly and compellingly. Optionally, share your writings with a trusted individual for feedback.

Combined Listening / Expressive Communication Exercises

Feedback Exchange

Objective: To practice giving and receiving feedback effectively.

Activity: With a partner, practice exchanging constructive feedback on a recent interaction or project. Focus on using "I" statements, being specific, and expressing appreciation for the feedback received, regardless of its nature.

Perspective-Sharing Circle

Objective: To develop empathy and understand diverse viewpoints.

Activity: Form a small group and select a topic for discussion. Each person shares their perspective on the topic, while others practice active listening. After everyone has spoken, discuss the different viewpoints without debating them, focusing on understanding and acknowledging each perspective.

Improvisational Speaking Games

Objective: To enhance quick thinking and adaptive communication.

Activity: Engage in improvisational speaking games, such as giving a spontaneous speech on a random topic or answering unexpected questions. Focus on staying coherent, engaging, and adapting your message on the fly.

By regularly practicing these exercises, you can significantly improve your active listening and expressive communication skills, leading to more effective and fulfilling interpersonal interactions.

5. Time Management

Mastering Your Moments for Maximum Impact

In the fast-paced world we navigate today, time management has become more than just a skill—it's an essential component of leading a productive, fulfilling life. Whether it's meeting professional deadlines, balancing personal commitments, or finding time for self-care, effective time management strategies can transform the way we live and work. This section of the book is dedicated to unraveling the complexities of managing one of our most precious resources: time.

Time management is about more than just schedules and to-do lists; it's about aligning our daily actions with our broader goals and values. By mastering time management, we can enhance our efficiency, reduce stress, and achieve a greater sense of satisfaction and well-being. This section will explore practical techniques and principles to help you effectively organize your time, prioritize tasks, and overcome procrastination and distractions.

Key Areas Covered:

Understanding the Importance of Time Management: We begin by examining why time management is crucial for success in all areas of life. Recognizing the value of your time is the first step toward making intentional choices about its use.

Setting Goals and Priorities: Learn how to set realistic, achievable goals that reflect your values and priorities. We'll introduce strategies for breaking down your goals into manageable tasks and prioritizing them effectively.

Planning and Scheduling: Discover tools and techniques for planning your days, weeks, and months to ensure you're focusing on the right tasks at the right time. From traditional planners to digital apps, find the system that works best for you.

Overcoming Procrastination: Delve into the psychological roots of procrastination and explore practical methods to overcome this common barrier to productivity. Learn how to motivate yourself to start tasks, maintain focus, and see them through to completion.

Managing Distractions: In an age of constant connectivity, distractions are everywhere. We'll cover strategies for minimizing interruptions and maintaining concentration, whether you're working in a busy office or from the quiet of your home.

Time Management Tools and Techniques: From the Pomodoro Technique to time blocking, discover a variety of methods that can help you use your time more effectively. Experiment with different approaches to find what works best for your lifestyle and work habits.

Achieving Work-Life Balance: Time management isn't just about being productive at work; it's also about making time for rest, relationships, and personal interests. Learn how to strike a balance that keeps you feeling fulfilled and energized.

Through practical advice, real-life examples, and actionable tips, this section aims to equip you with the knowledge and tools you need to take control of your time. By mastering time management, you can unlock your full potential, achieve your goals, and enjoy a more balanced, productive life. Let's embark on this journey together, transforming our relationship with time to make every moment count.

Understanding The Importance Of Time Management

Understanding the importance of time management is crucial in a world where demands on our time seem ever-increasing. Effective time management allows us to navigate our personal and professional lives more efficiently, reducing stress, enhancing productivity, and improving overall quality of life. By mastering the art of managing time, we can ensure that our daily activities align with our broader goals and values, enabling us to achieve more with our limited time.

Two popular methods for improving time management are the Pomodoro Technique and the Eisenhower Box (also known as the Eisenhower Matrix). Both offer unique approaches to organizing tasks and managing time effectively.

The Pomodoro Technique

The Pomodoro Technique, developed by Francesco Cirillo in the late 1980s, is a time management method that breaks work into intervals, traditionally 25 minutes in length, separated by short breaks. These intervals are known as "Pomodoros," named after the tomato-shaped kitchen timer Cirillo used as a university student.

How it works:

Choose a Task: Select a task you want to work on.

Set a Timer: Set a timer for 25 minutes and dedicate your focus to the task at hand.

Work Until the Timer Rings: Work on the task until the timer rings, then put a checkmark on a piece of paper.

Take a Short Break: Take a 5-minute break to relax and reset. This helps keep your mind fresh and focused.

Repeat: After four Pomodoros, take a longer break of 15-30 minutes.

Benefits: Enhances focus and concentration by encouraging short, intense work periods.

Reduces the impact of internal and external interruptions.

Increases awareness of how you spend your working time.

The Eisenhower Box

The Eisenhower Box, inspired by a quote attributed to Dwight D. Eisenhower, is a tool for prioritizing tasks based on their urgency and importance. It helps distinguish between tasks that require immediate attention and those that can be scheduled or delegated.

How it's structured:

The box is divided into four quadrants:

Urgent and Important (Do first): Tasks that require immediate attention.

Important, Not Urgent (Schedule): Tasks that are important but do not require immediate action.

Urgent, Not Important (Delegate): Tasks that need to be done soon but can be completed by someone else.

Neither Urgent nor Important (Eliminate): Tasks that do not contribute to your long-term goals or immediate well-being.

Benefits: Helps prioritize tasks by importance and urgency, ensuring that you focus on what truly matters.

Encourages delegation and the elimination of non-essential activities.

Clarifies decision-making about where to focus time and resources.

Both the Pomodoro Technique and the Eisenhower Box offer practical frameworks for managing time more effectively. By integrating these methods into your daily routine, you can enhance productivity, reduce stress, and create more space for personal and professional growth. Experimenting with these and other time management strategies can help you find the best approach to achieving balance and efficiency in your life.

Strategies For Managing Time More Effectively

Managing time effectively is a crucial skill that enhances productivity, reduces stress, and leads to more fulfilled personal and professional lives. However, even with the best intentions, many people find themselves procrastinating, which can undermine time management efforts. Understanding the psychology behind procrastination and employing strategies to manage time more effectively can help mitigate this common obstacle.

The Psychology of Procrastination

Procrastination is not simply a matter of poor time management or laziness but often stems from deeper psychological factors:

Fear of Failure: Avoiding tasks due to fear that the outcome will not meet high standards or expectations can lead to procrastination.

Perfectionism: The belief that everything must be perfect can be paralyzing, causing individuals to delay starting or completing tasks.

Overwhelm: Feeling overwhelmed by the size or complexity of a task can lead to avoidance behaviors.

Lack of Motivation: A disconnect between the task and personal goals or interests can reduce the incentive to begin or persist with a task.

Impulse Control: Difficulty in managing impulses can lead to prioritizing immediate gratification over long-term goals.

Strategies for Managing Time More Effectively

Break Tasks into Smaller Steps: Large tasks can seem overwhelming, leading to procrastination. Breaking them down into more manageable steps can reduce anxiety and make it easier to start.

Use the Two-Minute Rule: If a task takes less than two minutes, do it immediately. This rule helps clear small tasks that can accumulate and contribute to a sense of overwhelm.

Set Specific Goals: Vague goals are hard to achieve. Set specific, measurable, achievable, relevant, and time-bound (SMART) goals to provide clarity and direction.

Prioritize Tasks: Use tools like the Eisenhower Box to prioritize tasks based on their urgency and importance. Focus on what will have the most significant impact.

Eliminate Distractions: Identify what commonly distracts you (e.g., phone notifications, social media) and take steps to minimize these distractions when working on tasks.

Use Positive Reinforcement: Reward yourself for completing tasks, especially those you've been avoiding. Rewards can increase motivation and make it easier to tackle similar tasks in the future.

Practice Mindfulness and Self-Compassion: Be mindful of when you are procrastinating and explore the feelings driving this behavior without judgment. Practicing self-compassion can reduce the fear of failure and perfectionism that often underlies procrastination.

Seek Accountability: Share your goals with someone who will hold you accountable. Regular check-ins can provide additional motivation to complete tasks.

Develop a Routine: Establishing a consistent work routine can help automate task initiation, reducing the mental effort required to get started.

Visualize the Outcome: Spend a few moments visualizing the benefits of completing a task. This positive visualization can boost motivation and reduce procrastination.

By understanding the psychological roots of procrastination and applying these time management strategies, you can improve your ability to manage time effectively. These strategies not only help in combating procrastination but also enhance overall productivity and well-being.

Overcoming Procrastination And Distractions

Overcoming procrastination and distractions is essential for effective time management and achieving personal and professional goals. Procrastination, the act of delaying or postponing tasks, is often a symptom of deeper issues such as fear of failure, overwhelm, or a lack of motivation. Distractions, on the other hand, can divert focus from important tasks, further fueling procrastination. Here are practical steps to combat procrastination:

1. Acknowledge and Understand Your Procrastination

Begin by recognizing that you're procrastinating and try to understand why. Is it fear of failure, perfectionism, or perhaps the task seems too overwhelming? Identifying the root cause is the first step toward overcoming it.

2. Break Tasks into Smaller Steps

Large tasks can seem daunting and contribute to procrastination. Break them down into smaller, more manageable steps. This makes starting less intimidating and provides a clear path forward.

3. Set Clear Goals and Deadlines

Define what you want to achieve with each task and set specific, realistic deadlines. Use the SMART criteria (Specific, Measurable, Achievable, Relevant, Time-bound) to set goals that are clear and attainable.

4. Use the Five-Minute Rule

If you're struggling to start, commit to working on a task for just five minutes. Often, getting started is the hardest part, and once you've begun, you'll likely find it easier to continue.

5. Eliminate Distractions

Identify what commonly distracts you (e.g., phone, social media, emails) and take proactive steps to minimize these distractions when working. This might mean turning off notifications, using website blockers, or creating a dedicated workspace.

6. Prioritize Tasks

Use prioritization tools like the Eisenhower Box to determine which tasks are most important and urgent. Focus on completing these tasks first to ensure that your time is spent on high-priority activities.

7. Implement Time Management Techniques

Explore different time management techniques, such as the Pomodoro Technique or time blocking, to find what works best for you. These methods can help structure your time and make tasks more approachable.

8. Seek Support and Accountability

Share your goals with a friend, family member, or colleague who can help keep you accountable. Regular check-ins can provide motivation and support to keep you on track.

9. Reward Yourself

Set up a reward system for completing tasks or making significant progress. Rewards can provide additional motivation to overcome procrastination.

10. Practice Self-Compassion

Be kind to yourself when you encounter setbacks. Understand that procrastination is a common behavior and practice self-compassion rather than self-criticism, which can fuel further procrastination.

11. Visualize Success

Spend a few moments visualizing the positive outcomes of completing your tasks. This can help shift your focus from the fear of starting to the satisfaction of completion.

12. Adjust Your Environment

Create a workspace that minimizes distractions and is conducive to focus. This can mean different things for different people, so find an environment that works best for you.

Combating procrastination and distractions requires a multifaceted approach tailored to the underlying reasons for the behavior. By applying these practical steps, you can develop more effective time management skills, improve productivity, and achieve a greater sense of accomplishment.

Practice Exercises To Improve Time Management

Improving time management skills is essential for achieving both personal and professional goals, reducing stress, and enhancing overall quality of life. Here are practice exercises designed to help you develop a personalized time management plan and refine your ability to manage time effectively:

1. Time Audit

Objective: Identify how you currently spend your time to recognize areas for improvement.

Exercise: For one week, keep a detailed log of your daily activities and the time spent on each. Include work-related tasks, personal activities, and downtime.

Analysis: At the end of the week, review your log to identify patterns, time wasters, and activities that don't align with your priorities or goals.

2. Prioritization Exercise

Objective: Learn to prioritize tasks based on their importance and urgency.

Exercise: List all tasks you need to accomplish in a given week. Use the Eisenhower Box to categorize them into four quadrants: Urgent and Important, Important but Not Urgent, Urgent but Not Important, and Neither Urgent nor Important.

Application: Focus on completing tasks in the "Urgent and Important" category first, followed by scheduling time for "Important but Not Urgent" tasks. Delegate or minimize "Urgent but Not Important" tasks, and eliminate those in the "Neither" category.

3. Goal Setting and Breaking Down

Objective: Set achievable goals and break them down into manageable tasks.

Exercise: Identify a long-term goal you wish to achieve. Break it down into smaller, short-term goals, then list actionable steps for each short-term goal.

Implementation: Assign deadlines for each step and incorporate them into your daily or weekly schedule, ensuring they are realistic and achievable.

4. The Pomodoro Technique Trial

Objective: Improve focus and productivity by working in short, concentrated bursts.

Exercise: Choose a task and set a timer for 25 minutes (one Pomodoro). Work uninterrupted until the timer goes off, then take a 5-minute break. After four Pomodoros, take a longer break of 15-30 minutes.

Reflection: Note how many Pomodoros it takes to complete tasks and how your focus and productivity change using this method.

5. Weekly Planning Session

Objective: Develop a weekly schedule that balances work, personal commitments, and leisure.

Exercise: At the start of each week, spend 30 minutes planning your schedule. Allocate time for tasks based on priorities identified in the Prioritization Exercise. Include buffer times for unexpected tasks or delays.

Review: At the end of the week, review what was accomplished and adjust your planning strategy for the next week based on what worked and what didn't.

6. Time Blocking Method

Objective: Allocate specific blocks of time for different types of tasks to enhance focus and productivity.

Exercise: Divide your day into blocks of time, each dedicated to a specific type of task (e.g., emails, meetings, deep work). Stick to these blocks as closely as possible, adjusting as needed based on task urgency and importance.

Evaluation: Assess the effectiveness of this method in helping you complete tasks and maintain focus. Adjust your time blocks as necessary.

7. Daily Reflection and Adjustment

Objective: Reflect on daily accomplishments and challenges to continuously improve time management.

Exercise: Spend 10 minutes at the end of each day reflecting on what you accomplished, what challenges you faced, and how you can improve your time management the next day.

Adaptation: Use insights from this reflection to adjust your time management strategies and planning for the following day.

By incorporating these exercises into your routine, you can create a personalized time management plan that suits your unique needs and lifestyle. Regularly practicing and adjusting your approach will help you become more efficient, reduce stress, and achieve a better balance in your life.

6. Goal Setting

Charting Your Path to Success

Goal setting is a powerful process for envisioning your ideal future and for motivating yourself to turn your vision into reality. It is the act of identifying something you want to achieve and establishing measurable objectives and timeframes to help you achieve it. Effective goal setting enables you to focus your efforts, allocate your time and resources productively, and increase your chances of achieving what you want in life. Whether you're aiming to advance in your career, improve personal relationships, or acquire new skills, setting clear and achievable goals is a crucial first step.

This section of the book is dedicated to exploring the art and science of goal setting. It's designed to guide you through identifying your aspirations, setting specific, measurable, achievable, relevant, and time-bound (SMART) goals, and developing strategies to accomplish them. We'll delve into the psychological aspects that influence goal setting and achievement, such as motivation, mindset, and the importance of resilience in the face of setbacks.

Key Areas Covered:

Understanding Goal Setting: An introduction to the concept of goal setting, its importance, and its impact on personal and professional development.

Types of Goals: Differentiation between short-term, medium-term, and long-term goals, and how each plays a role in your overall strategy for success.

The SMART Criteria: A deep dive into creating SMART goals—those that are Specific, Measurable, Achievable, Relevant, and Time-bound—and how this framework can significantly enhance the clarity and attainability of your objectives.

Strategies for Successful Goal Achievement: Practical strategies and tips for setting yourself up for success, including planning, prioritization, and breaking larger goals into manageable tasks.

Overcoming Obstacles: Identifying common barriers to goal achievement, such as procrastination, fear of failure, and lack of motivation, and offering strategies to overcome these challenges.

Monitoring and Adjusting Your Goals: The importance of regularly reviewing your goals assessing your progress, and making adjustments as needed to stay on track.

Celebrating Success: Recognizing the importance of acknowledging and celebrating your achievements, which can provide additional motivation to pursue further goals.

Through practical advice, actionable tips, and motivational insights, this section aims to empower you to set meaningful goals and develop a clear plan for achieving them. Goal setting is not just about identifying what you want to achieve; it's about discovering who you want to become in the process. Let's embark on this journey together, setting sights on your aspirations and charting a path to turn your dreams into reality.

The Benefits Of Goal Setting

Goal setting is a fundamental practice that serves as a compass for personal and professional growth, guiding individuals towards achieving their aspirations. The benefits of goal setting are manifold, impacting various aspects of life by providing direction, motivation, and a sense of personal satisfaction. Furthermore, the SMART criteria—Specific, Measurable, Achievable, Relevant, Time-bound—have long been recognized as a powerful framework for setting effective goals. However, evolving perspectives on goal setting suggest that going beyond SMART goals can further enhance their effectiveness and adaptability to complex, changing environments.

Benefits of Goal Setting

Provides Clear Direction: Setting goals gives you a clear sense of direction. It helps prioritize activities and focus efforts on what is most important, steering your path towards desired outcomes.

Boosts Motivation: Goals act as motivational tools, encouraging you to put in the effort required to achieve them. They create a tangible vision of what success looks like, making the hard work feel more purposeful.

Enhances Time Management: By defining what you want to achieve, goal setting helps you better manage your time. You can allocate resources more efficiently and avoid wasting time on non-essential tasks.

Improves Decision-Making: Clear goals provide a criterion for making decisions by clarifying what is beneficial in the long term, thereby reducing indecision and procrastination.

Increases Resilience: By setting and pursuing goals, you develop perseverance and resilience. The process of overcoming obstacles and setbacks on the way to achieving your goals strengthens your ability to cope with challenges.

Fosters Personal Satisfaction: Achieving your goals provides a sense of accomplishment and personal satisfaction. It boosts self-esteem and confidence, motivating you to set new, challenging goals.

SMART Goals and Beyond

While the SMART criteria provide a solid foundation for goal setting, expanding beyond these principles can enhance their relevance and adaptability:

Meaningful and Motivating: Goals should not only be relevant but also meaningful to you personally. They should align with your values and passions to ensure intrinsic motivation.

Adaptable and Flexible: In a rapidly changing world, goals need to be adaptable. Be prepared to adjust your goals as circumstances change or as you gain more information.

Challenging Yet Achievable: While goals should be achievable, they should also stretch your abilities and encourage growth. Setting goals that are too easy might not provide enough motivation, while overly ambitious goals can lead to frustration.

Time-Bound with Milestones: In addition to setting deadlines, establish milestones along the way. These serve as checkpoints to assess progress, adjust course if necessary, and celebrate small wins.

Evaluate and Reflect: Regularly evaluate your progress towards your goals and reflect on what you're learning along the way. This reflective process can provide insights that inform future goal setting and personal development strategies.

By embracing the benefits of goal setting and adopting a comprehensive approach that goes beyond SMART goals, you can create a more dynamic, motivating, and fulfilling path towards achieving your aspirations. This holistic view encourages not just the achievement of specific outcomes but also personal growth and adaptability in the face of life's inevitable changes and challenges.

Setting Meaningful And Achievable Goals

Setting meaningful and achievable goals is a critical step toward personal and professional development. Goals that are both significant to the individual and realistically attainable drive motivation and provide a clear roadmap for success. Let's explore strategies used by successful individuals to set such goals, offering inspiration and practical guidance for your own goal-setting process.

Understand Your Why

Strategy: Successful individuals often start with a deep understanding of their "why" – the underlying purpose behind their goals. This understanding fuels motivation and resilience, making the goals more meaningful.

Example: Simon Sinek, author and motivational speaker, emphasizes starting with "why" to inspire action. By identifying the purpose behind your goals, you anchor them in something deeper, enhancing their significance and your commitment.

Set Goals Aligned with Your Values

Strategy: Aligning goals with personal values ensures they are meaningful and increases the likelihood of commitment and success.

Example: Oprah Winfrey, media mogul and philanthropist, has spoken about the importance of aligning her goals with her personal values of integrity and helping others. This alignment has guided her career decisions and philanthropic efforts, contributing to her lasting success.

Break Down Big Goals

Strategy: Breaking down large goals into smaller, manageable tasks makes them more achievable and less overwhelming.

Example: Jeff Bezos, founder of Amazon, focuses on "two-pizza teams" or small teams that can be fed with two pizzas, emphasizing the importance of small, agile teams in achieving broader company goals. This approach can be applied to personal goal setting by breaking down goals into smaller tasks that can be managed more effectively.

Embrace SMART Criteria

Strategy: Utilizing the SMART criteria (Specific, Measurable, Achievable, Relevant, Time-bound) ensures goals are well-defined and attainable.

Example: Sheryl Sandberg, COO of Facebook, advocates for setting clear, achievable goals, particularly in her approach to increasing women's leadership roles. By defining specific and measurable objectives, she and others can track progress and adjust strategies as needed.

Regularly Review and Adjust Goals

Strategy: Successful individuals regularly review their goals and are willing to adjust them based on progress, new information, or changes in circumstances.

Example: Elon Musk, CEO of SpaceX and Tesla, is known for setting ambitious goals and timelines. While not all goals are met within the original timelines, the process of regular review and adjustment keeps projects moving forward and innovating.

Visualize Success

Strategy: Visualization is a powerful tool for goal setting, helping to clarify the desired outcome and increase motivation.

Example: Visualization techniques have been used by athletes like Michael Phelps, the most decorated Olympian of all time. Phelps visualizes every aspect of his races, including potential challenges, which prepares him mentally to achieve his goals.

Build Accountability

Strategy: Sharing goals with others can create a sense of accountability, making it more likely that you'll follow through.

Example: Mark Zuckerberg, Facebook's CEO, has publicly shared personal challenges and goals, such as learning Mandarin or reading a new book every two weeks. This public commitment added a layer of accountability to his personal development efforts.

By adopting these strategies, you can set meaningful and achievable goals that propel you toward success. Remember, the process of setting and pursuing goals is as important as the outcomes, offering valuable opportunities for growth and learning along the way.

Staying Motivated And On Track

Staying motivated and on track with your goals can be challenging, especially when faced with obstacles, setbacks, or the day-to-day grind that can dull initial enthusiasm. However, implementing certain motivational strategies and techniques can significantly boost your ability to maintain focus and momentum. Here are practical and effective ways to keep yourself motivated and on track:

1. Set Clear, Achievable Goals

Technique: Use the SMART criteria to ensure your goals are Specific, Measurable, Achievable, Relevant, and Time-bound. Clear goals with defined steps make it easier to track progress and maintain motivation.

2. Break Down Goals into Smaller Tasks

Technique: Divide larger goals into smaller, manageable tasks. Celebrate completing these tasks to enjoy regular feelings of achievement, keeping motivation high.

3. Create a Visual Representation of Your Goals

Technique: Visualization boards or goal charts can serve as daily visual reminders of your goals. Seeing your goals and progress visually can boost motivation and commitment.

4. Find Your Why

Technique: Connect your goals to deeper values or purposes. Reminding yourself why a goal is important to you can reignite motivation, especially during challenging times.

5. Use Positive Affirmations

Technique: Positive affirmations can reinforce your belief in your ability to achieve your goals. Regularly recite affirmations that resonate with your goals and desired self-image.

6. Implement a Reward System

Technique: Set up rewards for reaching milestones. Rewards provide something tangible to look forward to and can significantly enhance motivation.

7. Maintain a Support System

Technique: Share your goals with friends, family, or a mentor who can offer support, encouragement, and accountability. Knowing you're not alone in your journey can be a powerful motivator.

8. Track and Celebrate Progress

Technique: Keep a log of your progress towards your goals. Reviewing this log can provide a motivational boost by highlighting how far you've come.

9. Adjust Goals as Needed

Technique: Be flexible and willing to adjust your goals based on feedback and changes in circumstances. Adaptability can prevent frustration and keep motivation levels high.

10. Engage in Regular Self-Reflection

Technique: Set aside time for regular self-reflection to assess your progress, address any challenges, and remind yourself of your achievements and learning.

11. Limit Distractions

Technique: Identify and minimize potential distractions that can derail your focus and motivation. Creating a dedicated workspace or time for working on your goals can help maintain focus.

12. Practice Self-Compassion

Technique: Be kind to yourself, especially when facing setbacks. Practice self-compassion to maintain a positive and motivated mindset, recognizing that setbacks are part of the journey.

13. Visualize Success

Technique: Regularly visualize achieving your goals. This mental rehearsal can enhance motivation and the belief in your ability to succeed.

By integrating these strategies and techniques into your routine, you can maintain motivation and stay on track with your goals, even when faced with challenges. Remember, motivation can ebb and flow, but with the right approaches, you can keep moving forward towards achieving your aspirations.

Practice Exercises To Improve Goal Setting Skills

Improving your goal-setting skills is crucial for personal and professional development. Effective goal setting helps you focus your acquisition of knowledge, and it organizes your time and resources so that you can make the most of your life. Here are practice exercises that include goal-mapping and progress tracking, designed to enhance your ability to set and achieve your goals effectively.

Exercise 1: Define Your Vision and Set Long-Term Goals

Objective: To create a clear vision of your ideal future and set long-term goals that align with this vision.

Activity: Write a detailed description of where you see yourself in 5 to 10 years. Consider all aspects of your life, including career, personal development, relationships, and health.

Follow-Up: From this vision, identify 3 to 5 long-term goals that are crucial for making this vision a reality. Use the SMART criteria to refine these goals.

Exercise 2: Create a Goal-Mapping Template

Objective: To break down long-term goals into medium-term objectives and short-term actions.

Activity: For each long-term goal, identify 2 to 3 medium-term objectives (achievable in 1 to 2 years) that will progress you towards your goal. Then, for each medium-term objective, list out short-term actions (achievable in the next 3 to 6 months).

Template Structure: Create a visual template that maps these components. It could be a flowchart, a mind map, or a hierarchical list, whichever format you find most helpful.

Exercise 3: Develop a Progress Tracking Template

Objective: To monitor your progress towards your goals effectively.

Activity: Design a progress tracking template that includes:

Goal/Objective Name: The name of your long-term goal or medium-term objective.

Milestone: Key milestones or short-term actions needed to achieve the objective.

Deadline: When you aim to complete each milestone.

Status: Current progress status (Not Started, In Progress, Completed).

Notes: Any relevant notes, obstacles encountered, or adjustments made.

Application: Use this template weekly or monthly to review your progress, identify any areas where you're falling behind, and adjust your plan as necessary.

Exercise 4: Set and Review Weekly Goals

Objective: To maintain momentum and continuously make progress towards your long-term goals.

Activity: At the beginning of each week, set specific goals you aim to achieve by the end of the week. These should be actions that move you closer to your medium-term objectives.

Review Session: At the end of the week, hold a review session to assess your progress. Note what was accomplished, what wasn't, and why. Use this information to plan more effectively for the next week.

Exercise 5: Reflective Journaling

Objective: To develop insights into your goal-setting and achievement process.

Activity: Keep a reflective journal where you regularly document your thoughts, feelings, successes, and challenges related to your goals.

Questions for Reflection:

What did I learn about myself this week/month?
What obstacles did I encounter, and how did I overcome them?
How can I improve my approach to achieving my goals?

By engaging in these exercises, you'll not only refine your goal-setting skills but also enhance your ability to track progress and adjust your strategies as needed. This holistic approach to goal setting and achievement will empower you to realize your vision for the future, one goal at a time.

7. Mindfulness

The Path to Presence and Clarity

In today's fast-paced world, where distractions abound and the pressure to perform is ever-present, mindfulness emerges as a beacon of tranquility and focus. Mindfulness is the practice of being fully present and engaged in the moment, aware of your thoughts and feelings without distraction or judgment. It is about experiencing life as it unfolds, with openness and curiosity, rather than being caught up in the whirlwind of thoughts about the past or the future.

This section of the book delves into the essence of mindfulness, exploring its principles, benefits, and the myriad ways it can be integrated into daily ife. Mindfulness is not just a practice but a way of being that can enhance every aspect of your existence, from improving mental ard physical health to deepening relationships and boosting productivity.

Key Areas Covered:

The Foundations of Mindfulness: Understanding what mindfulness is and its roots in ancient practices. This includes exploring the mind-body connection and how mindfulness can alter our engagement with the world.

Benefits of Mindfulness: A look at the extensive research highlighting the positive impacts of mindfulness on mental health, stress reduction, emotional regulation, and overall well-being.

Practical Mindfulness Techniques: An introduction to various mindfulness exercises and techniques, including mindful breathing

, meditation, and body scans. These practices are designed to cultivate a state of mindful awareness in everyday activities.

Mindfulness in Daily Life: Strategies for incorporating mindfulness into routine activities to enhance presence and awareness. This includes mindful eating, walking, and listening, transforming mundane tasks into opportunities for mindfulness practice.

Overcoming Challenges with Mindfulness: How mindfulness can be used as a tool to navigate life's challenges, including stress, anxiety, and chronic pain. It offers a pathway to resilience, equipping individuals with the skills to face difficulties with grace and equanimity.

Mindfulness and Relationships: Exploring the role of mindfulness in enhancing communication and deepening connections with others. Mindful listening and speaking can foster more meaningful and compassionate interactions.

Advanced Mindfulness Practices: For those looking to deepen their mindfulness journey, this section covers more advanced practices and concepts, such as loving-kindness meditation and mindfulness retreats.

Building a Mindful Lifestyle: Tips for creating a lifestyle that supports and nurtures mindfulness, including creating spaces for practice, establishing routines, and connecting with a community of like-minded individuals.

Through practical advice, guided practices, and real-life applications, this section aims to introduce you to the transformative power of mindfulness. Whether you are new to mindfulness or looking to deepen your practice, you will find valuable insights and techniques to help you live more mindfully. Embracing mindfulness is a journey towards a more present, peaceful, and fulfilling life, inviting you to experience each moment fully and with intention. Let's embark on this path together, exploring the profound benefits mindfulness offers to our lives and well-being.

Understanding Mindfulness And Its Benefits

Mindfulness, a practice rooted in ancient meditation traditions, has gained widespread recognition in contemporary psychology and wellness communities for its profound benefits on mental and physical health. At its core, mindfulness involves paying attention to the present moment with an attitude of openness, curiosity, and non-judgment. This simple yet powerful practice encourages individuals to observe their thoughts, feelings, and bodily sensations as they arise, without getting caught up in them. The science behind mindfulness reveals why and how this practice can lead to significant improvements in well-being, stress reduction, and overall quality of life.

The Science Behind Mindfulness

Neuroplasticity and Mindfulness: Research has shown that regular mindfulness practice can lead to changes in brain structure and function, a phenomenon known as neuroplasticity. Studies using MRI scans have found increased gray matter density in areas of the brain associated with memory, learning, and emotion regulation, such as the hippocampus and prefrontal cortex, in individuals who practice mindfulness meditation regularly. Additionally, reductions in the amygdala's size, the region related to stress and fear responses, have been observed, indicating a decrease in emotional reactivity.

Stress Reduction: One of the most well-documented benefits of mindfulness is its ability to reduce stress. The practice helps individuals shift their response to stress from a reactive fight-or-flight mode to a more reflective stance, thereby lowering cortisol levels and reducing the overall physiological impact of stress on the body. Mindfulness-based stress reduction (MBSR) programs have been particularly effective in teaching individuals how to cope with stress in healthier ways.

Emotional Regulation: Mindfulness enhances emotional regulation by improving the ability to observe and identify emotions without immediately reacting to them. This increased emotional awareness allows for more thoughtful responses to challenging situations, rather than being driven by automatic, often negative, emotional patterns. The practice has been linked to reduced symptoms of anxiety and depression, as well as improved mood and well-being.

Attention and Concentration: Regular mindfulness practice improves concentration and attention. By training the mind to focus on the present moment, individuals can enhance their ability to maintain attention over longer periods. This has implications for productivity and the ability to engage deeply with tasks without being easily distracted.

Physical Health Benefits: Beyond mental health, mindfulness has been shown to have positive effects on physical health. These include lower blood pressure, improved immune function, and reduced chronic pain. The practice can also support healthier lifestyle choices, such as improved sleep patterns and dietary habits.

Interpersonal Relationships: Mindfulness can positively affect relationships through improved empathy and compassion. By becoming more attuned to their own emotions and reactions, individuals can better understand and relate to others' feelings and perspectives, leading to more meaningful and supportive interactions.

Integrating Mindfulness

Given its extensive benefits, integrating mindfulness into daily life can be a valuable practice for anyone looking to enhance their well-being. This can be achieved through formal meditation practices as well as informal mindfulness exercises, such as mindful walking, eating, or listening, making mindfulness an accessible tool for improving quality of life.

The growing body of scientific evidence supporting the benefits of mindfulness underscores its value as a practice for mental and physical health. As research continues to reveal the mechanisms behind mindfulness, it becomes increasingly clear that this ancient practice offers profound benefits for contemporary life, encouraging a balanced, reflective, and engaged approach to living.

Integrating Mindfulness Into Daily Life

Integrating mindfulness into daily life can transform routine activities into opportunities for increased awareness, presence, and tranquility. Whether you have only a few minutes or can dedicate a longer period to practice, mindfulness can be woven into the fabric of your day. Below are guided mindfulness exercises and resources to help you cultivate mindfulness throughout your daily activities.

1. Mindful Breathing

Exercise: This can be done anywhere, anytime. Simply focus your attention on your breath. Notice the sensation of air entering and exiting your nostrils, or the rise and fall of your chest. When your mind wanders, gently bring your focus back to your breath. Start with one minute and gradually increase the duration.

2. Mindful Eating

Exercise: Turn mealtime into a mindfulness practice. Begin by observing your food, noticing colors, textures, and aromas. Chew slowly, savoring each bite and paying attention to the flavors and sensations in your mouth. This practice enhances the eating experience and can improve digestion.

3. Mindful Walking

Exercise: Next time you walk, whether it's a short walk from your car to the office or a longer stroll in nature, engage in mindful walking. Focus on the sensation of your feet touching the ground, the rhythm of your steps, and the feeling of the air on your skin. Observe the sights and sounds around you without judgment.

4. Body Scan Meditation

Exercise: Lie down or sit comfortably. Close your eyes and bring your attention to your body. Starting at your toes and moving upwards, slowly focus on each part of your body in turn. Notice any sensations, tension, or discomfort. Breathe into these areas and imagine the tension releasing with each exhale.

5. Mindful Listening

Exercise: In conversations, practice fully focusing on the speaker.

Notice their words, tone, and body language. Resist the urge to formulate your response while they're speaking. Instead, listen with openness and curiosity. This not only improves relationships but also enhances your understanding and empathy.

6. Pause and Observe

Exercise: Several times a day, take a brief pause from what you're doing. Look around and notice five things you can see, four things you can touch, three things you can hear, two things you can smell, and one thing you can taste. This simple exercise can quickly bring you back to the present moment.

Resources for Further Practice

Mindfulness Apps: Apps like "Headspace," "Calm," and "Insight Timer" offer guided meditations, mindfulness exercises, and educational content to support your practice.

Books: "Wherever You Go, There You Are" by Jon Kabat-Zinn and "The Miracle of Mindfulness" by Thich Nhat Hanh provide deep insights into mindfulness practice and its benefits.

Online Courses: Platforms like Coursera and Udemy offer courses on mindfulness and meditation, ranging from introductory to advanced levels, taught by experienced practitioners.

Local Meditation Groups: Joining a meditation group or attending mindfulness workshops can provide support and deepen your practice through community learning.

Integrating mindfulness into daily life doesn't require drastic changes to your routine. Instead, it involves bringing a mindful awareness to the activities you're already doing. Over time, these practices can lead to significant improvements in your mental and physical well-being, enhancing your overall quality of life.

The Benefits Of Mindfulness Meditation

Mindfulness meditation is a practice that involves focusing one's attention on the present moment, observing thoughts, feelings, bodily sensations, and the surrounding environment with openness, curiosity, and non-judgment. This form of meditation has roots in Buddhist traditions but has been widely adopted across cultures due to its universal benefits for mental and physical health. Here, we explore the benefits of mindfulness meditation and introduce a variety of techniques to incorporate into your practice.

Benefits of Mindfulness Meditation

Reduces Stress: Regular mindfulness meditation has been shown to decrease stress levels by lowering cortisol, the body's stress hormone. It helps in developing a more balanced response to stressors.

Improves Emotional Well-being: Practicing mindfulness can lead to reductions in anxiety, depression, and emotional reactivity, while enhancing positive emotions and the sense of well-being.

Enhances Focus and Concentration: Mindfulness meditation improves the ability to maintain attention and focus, which can enhance productivity and learning efficiency.

Boosts Immune System: Studies suggest that mindfulness meditation can lead to improved immune function, helping the body to better resist illnesses.

Improves Sleep: By reducing stress and promoting relaxation, mindfulness meditat on can improve sleep patterns and help combat insomnia.

Fosters Compassion and Empathy: Mindfulness practices that focus on loving-kindness and compassion can increase feelings of empathy and connectedness to others.

Enhances Self-awareness: Regular practice leads to greater insight into one's thoughts, feelings, and behaviors, promoting personal growth and self-understanding.

Variety of Mindfulness Meditation Techniques

Breath Awareness Meditation:

Focus solely on your breath, observing each inhalation and exhalation. Notice the rise and fall of your chest, or the sensation of air passing through your nostrils. When your mind wanders, gently redirect your attention back to your breath.

Body Scan Meditation:

Lie down or sit comfortably. Starting from your toes and moving upwards, bring your attention to each part of your body in turn. Observe any sensaticns, tension, or discomfort without judgment, breathing into these areas and imagining the tension releasing.

Walking Meditation:

Engage in mindful walking by focusing on the physical experience of walking. Pay attention to the sensation of your feet touching the ground, the rhythm of your steps, and your breathing. This can be practiced in a quiet room or outdoors in nature.

Loving-Kindness Meditation (Metta):

Begin by directing feelings of love and kindness towards yourself, then gradually extend these feelings to loved ones, acquaintances, and even those with whom you have difficulties. Use phrases like "May I/you be happy, may I/you be healthy, may I/you live with ease."

Mindful Eating:

Transform eating into a mindfulness practice by eating slowly and without distraction. Observe the colors, textures, and smells of your food, and savor each bite, paying attention to the taste and sensations in your mouth.

Object Meditation:

Focus your attention on a single object, such as a candle flame or a flower. Observe it in detail, noticing its colors, shapes, and textures, and any thoughts or feelings that arise.

Sound Meditation:

Close your eyes and focus on the sounds around you. Listen without labeling or judging the sounds, simply experiencing them as they are.

Incorporating mindfulness meditation into your daily routine can lead to profound improvements in your mental, emotional, and physical health. Experiment with different techniques to find the practices that resonate most with you, and remember that the key to mindfulness is regular, consistent practice.

Practice Exercises To Improve Mindfulness

Incorporating mindfulness into your daily life can significantly enhance your awareness, reduce stress, and improve overall well-being. Engaging in specific mindfulness exercises can help cultivate this skill. Below are practice exercises designed to improve mindfulness, including daily challenge activities to integrate mindfulness into your routine.

1. Mindful Morning Routine

Exercise: Start your day with mindfulness by engaging fully in your morning routine. Whether it's brushing your teeth, showering, or having breakfast, focus entirely on the activity you're doing. Notice the sensations, textures, tastes, and smells. If your mind wanders, gently bring your attention back to the task at hand.

Daily Challenge: Each morning, choose one routine activity to perform mindfully.

2. Mindful Breathing Breaks

Exercise: Several times throughout the day, take a one-minute mindful breathing break. Focus on the sensation of breath entering and leaving your body. Notice the rise and fall of your chest or the feeling of air passing through your nostrils. When thoughts arise, acknowledge them and return your focus to your breath.

Daily Challenge: Set reminders to take mindful breathing breaks, especially during times of stress or transition between tasks.

3. Mindful Observation

Exercise: Select an object from your surroundings and spend a few minutes observing it with your full attention. It could be a plant, a cup of coffee, or anything else within your sight. Notice the details of its color, texture, and shape. Observe it as if you're seeing it for the first time.

Daily Challenge: Choose a different object to observe mindfully each day.

4. Mindful Listening

Exercise: Engage in mindful listening during conversations. Focus entirely on the speaker, paying attention to their words, tone, and body language. Resist the urge to formulate your response while they're speaking. Instead, listen with openness and curiosity.

Daily Challenge: Practice mindful listening in at least one conversation per day.

5. Mindful Eating

Exercise: Dedicate at least one meal or snack per day to mindful eating. Before eating, observe the food, noting its colors, smells, and textures. Chew slowly, savoring each bite and paying attention to the flavors and sensations in your mouth.

Daily Challenge: Try to introduce mindful eating into more meals throughout the day.

6. Mindful Walking

Exercise: Take a short, mindful walk each day. Focus on the sensation of your feet touching the ground, the movement of your body, and the air on your skin. Observe the sights and sounds around you without judgment.

Daily Challenge: Incorporate a brief mindful walk into your daily routine, even if it's just for a few minutes.

7. Gratitude Reflection

Exercise: End your day by reflecting on three things you're grateful for. It could be experiences from the day, personal attributes, people in your life, or anything else. Focusing on gratitude can shift your attention to positive aspects of your life, fostering a sense of well-being.

Daily Challenge: Write down your gratitude reflections in a journal each night.

8. Body Scan Meditation

Exercise: Practice a body scan meditation before bed. Lie down in a comfortable position and slowly bring your attention to different parts of your body, from your toes to your head. Notice any sensations, tension, or discomfort without judgment. Breathe into these areas, imagining the tension releasing with each exhale.

Daily Challenge: Make body scan meditation a part of your nightly routine to promote relaxation and mindfulness at the end of the day.

By engaging in these exercises and challenges, you can weave mindfulness into the fabric of your daily life, enhancing your ability to live in the present moment with greater awareness and appreciation.

8. Stress Management

Navigating Life's Pressures with Grace and Resilience

In our fast-paced, ever-changing world, stress has become a ubiquitous part of life. While a certain level of stress can be motivating and help us meet daily challenges, too much stress, or chronic stress, can be detrimental to our physical, mental, and emotional well-being. Managing stress effectively is, therefore, not just about enhancing our capacity to cope with life's demands but also about improving our overall quality of life. This section of the book delves into the art and science of stress management, offering insights, strategies, and practical exercises to help you navigate life's pressures with grace and resilience.

Understanding stress and its impact on the body and mind is the first step toward effective management. Stress triggers the body's "fight or flight" response, releasing hormones like cortisol and adrenaline, which prepare us to act. While this response can be life-saving in emergency situations, prolonged activation can lead to health issues, including anxiety, depression, heart disease, and a weakened immune system.

Key Areas Covered:

Understanding Stress: An exploration of what stress is, its causes, and its effects on the body and mind. This foundation is crucial for recognizing stressors in your own life and how they impact you.

Identifying Personal Stressors: Techniques and exercises to help you identify your unique stress triggers. Understanding your personal stressors is essential for developing targeted strategies to manage them.

Physical Stress-Relief Techniques: Practical methods to alleviate physical symptoms of stress, including deep breathing exercises, progressive muscle relaxation, and physical activity. These techniques can help reduce the physiological effects of stress, promoting relaxation and well-being.

Cognitive and Emotional Strategies: Cognitive-behavioral strategies and mindfulness practices that address the mental and emotional aspects of stress. This includes reframing negative thoughts, practicing mindfulness and meditation, and developing emotional resilience.

Lifestyle Adjustments for Stress Reduction: Guidance on making lifestyle changes that can reduce stress levels, such as improving sleep habits, adopting a healthy diet, and managing time effectively. Small adjustments can have a significant impact on your overall stress levels.

Building a Support System: The importance of social support in stress management. Strategies for strengthening relationships, seeking support when needed, and the benefits of sharing your experiences with others.

Creating a Personal Stress Management Plan: Steps to develop a comprehensive and personalized plan to manage stress. This plan combines techniques and strategies that resonate with you, tailored to fit your lifestyle and address your specific stressors.

Preventive Strategies: Approaches to prevent stress from building up in the first place, including setting boundaries, practicing regular self-care, and maintaining a balance between work and leisure activities.

Through a combination of theoretical insights and practical exercises, this section equips you with the tools and knowledge to manage stress effectively. By adopting a proactive approach to stress management, you can enhance your resilience, improve your health and well-being, and navigate life's challenges with a sense of calm and confidence. Let's embark on this journey together, learning to master stress management techniques that will serve you well throughout life's ups and downs.

Understanding The Impact Of Stress

Understanding the impact of stress and identifying personal stress triggers are critical steps in developing effective stress management strategies. Stress, a natural response to perceived threats or challenges, can be beneficial in short bursts, helping us to react quickly or meet pressing deadlines. However, when stress becomes chronic, it can have significant adverse effects on our physical, emotional, and mental health.

The Impact of Stress

Physical Health: Chronic stress can lead to a host of physical health problems, including high blood pressure, heart disease, obesity, diabetes, and a weakened immune system. It can also exacerbate existing health conditions.

Mental Health: Prolonged stress is a key factor in the development of anxiety disorders, depression, and other mental health issues. It can impair concentration, decision-making, and memory.

Emotional Well-being: High levels of stress can lead to emotional imbalances, manifesting as irritability, frustration, overwhelm, and a general sense of being unable to cope with daily life.

Behavioral Changes: Stress can affect behavior, leading to unhealthy coping mechanisms such as overeating, under-eating, alcohol or drug abuse, and social withdrawal.

Identifying Personal Stress Triggers

Personal stress triggers vary widely among individuals, influenced by personality, life experiences, and current circumstances. Identifying your specific triggers is essential for managing stress effectively. Common stressors include:

Work-related Stress: Deadlines, workload, job security, and interpersonal conflicts at work.

Personal Relationships: Difficulties in relationships with family, friends, or romantic partners.

Life Changes: Major life changes, such as moving, changing jobs, or dealing with loss.

Financial Concerns: Worries about money, debt, and financial security.

Health Issues: Personal health problems or caring for someone with health issues.

Exercise for Identifying Stress Triggers: Keep a stress journal for a week or two. Note down instances when you feel stressed, including the context, your thoughts, emotional reactions, and how you responded. Over time, patterns will emerge, helping you identify your primary stress triggers.

Strategies for Managing Stress

Once you've identified your stress triggers, you can develop targeted strategies to manage them. Effective stress management involves a combination of lifestyle changes, cognitive strategies, and relaxation techniques.

Lifestyle Changes:

Exercise Regularly: Physical activity can reduce stress hormones and trigger the release of endorphins, improving your mood.

Healthy Eating: A balanced diet can impact your mood and energy levels, influencing how you handle stress.

Adequate Sleep: Ensure you get enough restful sleep, as lack of sleep can exacerbate stress.

Cognitive Strategies:

Reframe Your Thoughts: Practice identifying and challenging negative thought patterns, replacing them with more positive, realistic ones.

Set Realistic Goals: Break tasks into manageable steps and set achievable goals to avoid feeling overwhelmed.

Relaxation Techniques:

Deep Breathing Exercises: Practice breathing techniques to help calm your mind and body.

Mindfulness and Meditation: Regular mindfulness practice can increase your awareness of stress triggers and your reactions to them, helping you manage stress more effectively.

Progressive Muscle Relaxation: Learn to tense and then slowly release each muscle group in your body, promoting physical and mental relaxation.

Build a Support Network: Share your feelings with trusted friends, family, or a professional counselor. Social support is vital in managing stress.

By understanding the impact of stress and identifying your personal triggers, you can take proactive steps to manage stress effectively. Integrating these strategies into your daily routine can help mitigate the adverse effects of stress, leading to improved health, happiness, and overall quality of life.

Techniques For Reducing Stress

While traditional stress reduction techniques like deep breathing, exercise, and time management are widely known and practiced, exploring alternative methods can offer fresh perspectives and new tools for managing stress. These alternative techniques cater to diverse preferences and lifestyles, providing a broad spectrum of options for reducing stress. Here's a look at some unique and effective alternative stress reduction techniques:

1. Aromatherapy

Description: Uses essential oils derived from plants to promote relaxation and well-being through inhalation or skin absorption.

How to Use: Diffuse lavender, chamomile, or sandalwood essential oils in your living space or apply diluted oils to pulse points for a calming effect.

2. Art Therapy

Description: Involves engaging in creative activities like drawing, painting, or sculpting as a way to express and understand emotions.

How to Use: Set aside time for creative expression without judgment or aim. Focus on the process rather than the outcome to facilitate stress relief.

3. Forest Bathing (Shinrin-yoku)

Description: A Japanese practice of spending time in nature, particularly forests, to enhance health, wellness, and happiness.

How to Use: Visit a nearby forest or natural area and spend time walking slowly, observing the environment with all your senses to reduce stress and improve mood.

4. Laughter Yoga

Description: Combines laughter exercises with yogic breathing to promote health and well-being.

How to Use: Join a laughter yoga class or practice laughing heartily for a few minutes at home, even if it starts with forced laughter. It often leads to genuine laughter, releasing endorphins and reducing stress.

5. Biofeedback

Description: A technique that teaches you how to control physiological functions, such as heart rate and muscle tension, through real-time feedback from monitoring devices.

How to Use: With the help of a trained professional, learn to control specific body processes that are normally involuntary, reducing physical symptoms of stress.

6. EFT Tapping (Emotional Freedom Techniques)

Description: Combines elements of cognitive therapy with acupressure to address emotional and physical pain.

How to Use: Tap on specific meridian points on the body while focusing on a particular issue or stressor to help release emotional tension.

7. Tai Chi or Qigong

Description: Chinese practices that combine slow, deliberate movements, meditation, and breathing exercises to enhance physical and mental health.

How to Use: Join a class or follow online tutorials to practice these gentle martial arts, which can help reduce stress, improve balance, and promote a sense of calm.

8. Sound Therapy

Description: Uses aspects of music or sound vibrations to improve physical and emotional health and well-being.

How to Use: Listen to binaural beats, gongs, singing bowls, or nature sounds to relax and reduce stress. Participating in drumming circles can also be therapeutic.

9. Guided Imagery

Description: Involves visualizing a peaceful scene or scenario in great detail to promote relaxation.

How to Use: Listen to guided imagery recordings or practice independently by imagining yourself in a serene location, focusing on the sensory experiences to distract from stress.

10. Journaling for Gratitude

Description: Writing down things you are grateful for to shift focus from stressors to positive aspects of life.

How to Use: Keep a gratitude journal and write down three things you're thankful for each day. This practice can improve mood and reduce stress by changing your perspective.

Exploring these alternative stress reduction techniques can provide valuable additions to your stress management toolkit, offering diverse ways to relax, rejuvenate, and maintain balance in the face of life's challenges.

Improving Resilience And Coping Skills

Improving resilience and coping skills is essential for navigating life's challenges effectively. Resilience, the ability to bounce back from setbacks, adapt to change, and keep going in the face of adversity, can be developed and strengthened over time. Coping skills are the strategies individuals use to manage stressful situations and emotions. Personalizing these strategies can make them more effective, as they cater to individual preferences, strengths, and life circumstances. Here's a guide to developing personalized coping strategies that enhance resilience:

1. Self-Assessment

Objective: Identify your current coping mechanisms and evaluate their effectiveness.

Activity: Reflect on recent stressful situations and jot down how you responded to them. Categorize these responses into helpful and unhelpful coping strategies.

2. Recognize Your Stressors

Objective: Identify specific stressors in your life to target your coping strategies effectively.

Activity: Keep a stress diary for a few weeks, noting what causes you stress, how you feel, and how you respond. Look for patterns to identify your primary stressors.

3. Build on Your Strengths

Objective: Utilize your personal strengths to enhance your resilience.

Activity: Take a strengths-finding quiz or reflect on past challenges you've overcome. Consider how your strengths helped you cope and how they can be applied to current stressors.

4. Develop a Toolkit of Coping Strategies

Objective: Create a personalized set of coping strategies based on your self-assessment and strengths.

Activity: Compile a list of coping strategies that align with your strengths and preferences. This could include physical activities (e.g., exercise, yoga), relaxation techniques (e.g., meditation, deep breathing), creative outlets (e.g., art, music), and social activities (e.g., spending time with loved ones, volunteering).

5. Practice Mindfulness and Emotional Regulation

Objective: Improve awareness and management of emotions.

Activity: Incorporate mindfulness practices into your daily routine, such as mindful breathing or meditation. When faced with stress, practice identifying and labeling your emotions to manage them more effectively.

6. Set Realistic Goals

Objective: Foster a sense of achievement and progress.

Activity: Break down overwhelming tasks into smaller, achievable goals. Celebrate small victories to build confidence and motivation.

7. Cultivate a Positive Outlook

Objective: Develop optimism and a positive approach to challenges.

Activity: Practice reframing negative thoughts into positive ones. Use gratitude journaling to focus on the positive aspects of your life.

8. Foster Social Connections

Objective: Build a support network for emotional and practical support.

Activity: Invest time in strengthening relationships with family and friends. Consider joining support groups or community activities to expand your social network.

9. Learn from Experience

Objective: Use past experiences to inform future coping strategies.

Activity: Reflect on how you've successfully coped with stress in the past. Consider what strategies worked well and how they can be adapted or improved for future challenges.

10. Seek Professional Help When Needed

Objective: Recognize when additional support is needed.

Activity: If stress becomes overwhelming, consider seeking support from a mental health professional who can provide guidance and additional coping strategies.

By understanding your unique stressors and leveraging your strengths, you can develop a personalized set of coping strategies that enhance your resilience. Remember, resilience is not about never facing difficulties but about navigating through them effectively. With practice and persistence, you can build the skills needed to thrive in the face of life's challenges.

Practice Exercises For Stress Management

Effective stress management is crucial for maintaining both physical and mental health. By incorporating specific practice exercises into your daily routine, you can learn to manage stress more effectively. Here are several exercises, including the use of a stress diary and various relaxation techniques, to help you in managing stress.

1. Keeping a Stress Diary

Objective: To identify stress triggers and patterns in your responses to stress.

Exercise: For two weeks, keep a detailed diary of moments when you feel stressed. Note the date, time, place, what you were doing, who you were with, how you felt both physically and emotionally, and how you responded to the stress. After two weeks, review your diary to identify common triggers and your reactions to them.

Follow-Up: Use this information to develop strategies for avoiding these triggers or changing your response to them in the future.

2. Deep Breathing Exercises

Objective: To use breath control to reduce stress and elicit the body's relaxation response.

Exercise: Sit or lie down in a comfortable position. Close your eyes, and take a deep breath in through your nose, allowing your stomach to rise as you fill your lungs with air. Hold the breath for a few seconds, then slowly exhale through your mouth, letting your stomach fall. Repeat for 3-5 minutes.

Follow-Up: Practice deep breathing daily, or whenever you feel stress levels rising.

3. Progressive Muscle Relaxation (PMR)

Objective: To relieve muscle tension associated with stress.

Exercise: Begin by finding a quiet place where you can sit or lie down comfortably. Tense a group of muscles as you breathe in, squeezing them as tightly as you can. Hold for a few seconds, then relax the muscles as you breathe out. Work your way through all major muscle groups, starting from your feet and moving up to your face.

Follow-Up: Incorporate PMR into your evening routine to reduce stress and improve sleep.

4. Mindfulness Meditation

Objective: To cultivate awareness of the present moment, reducing stress and enhancing overall well-being.

Exercise: Find a quiet space and sit comfortably with your eyes closed. Focus on your breath, the rise and fall of your chest, or the sensation of air flowing in and out of your nostrils. When your mind wanders, gently bring your attention back to your breath without judgment.

Follow-Up: Aim to practice mindfulness meditation for 5-10 minutes daily, gradually increasing the duration as you become more comfortable with the practice.

5. Guided Imagery

Objective: To use visualization to induce relaxation and reduce stress.

Exercise: In a quiet space, close your eyes and imagine a peaceful setting that makes you feel relaxed and happy. It could be a beach, a garden, or any place you find serene. Focus on the details of this place—the sights, sounds, smells, and how it makes you feel. Spend 5-10 minutes immersing yourself in this visualization.

Follow-Up: Practice guided imagery whenever you need a quick stress relief or before bedtime to improve sleep.

6. Physical Activity

Objective: To use exercise as a way to reduce stress hormones and produce endorphins, the body's natural mood elevators.

Exercise: Incorporate physical activity into your daily routine, whether it's a brisk walk, a yoga session, or a workout at the gym. Aim for at least 30 minutes of moderate exercise most days of the week.

Follow-Up: Set specific, achievable goals for your physical activity, and track your progress to stay motivated.

By regularly practicing these exercises, you can develop a more proactive approach to managing stress, leading to improved health, mood, and quality of life. Remember, the key to effective stress management is consistency and finding the right combination of techniques that work for you.

9. Personal Habits

Personal Habits: The Building Blocks of a Fulfilling Life

Personal habits, the small, repeated actions we perform daily, wield immense power over every aspect of our lives. From the moment we wake to the time we retire at night, our habits shape our health, productivity, happiness, and overall quality of life. Recognizing and understanding the impact of these habits provides a foundation for personal growth and development. This section delves into the significance of cultivating positive personal habits and offers strategies for transforming detrimental habits into life-enhancing practices.

Habits are formed through repetition and, over time, become automatic responses that require minimal conscious thought. While this can lead to the effortless maintenance of beneficial routines, it can also make unhelpful habits difficult to break. The key to a fulfilling life often lies in the delicate balance of maintaining positive habits while identifying and altering those that hold us back.

Key Areas Covered:

The Science of Habit Formation: An exploration of how habits are formed in the brain, the role of cues, routines, and rewards in reinforcing habits, and strategies for leveraging this knowledge to change behaviors.

Assessing Personal Habits: Techniques for identifying and evaluating your current habits, distinguishing between those that contribute to your goals and those that detract from them.

Building Positive Habits: Practical steps for establishing new, beneficial habits. This includes setting clear intentions, creating a supportive environment, and leveraging small changes for big impacts.

Breaking Negative Habits: Strategies for overcoming barriers to habit change, such as understanding the triggers and rewards that sustain unwanted behaviors and replacing them with healthier alternatives.

The Role of Mindfulness in Habit Change: How mindfulness and self-awareness can support the process of habit modification by increasing recognition of habits and their effects on our lives.

Maintaining Habits: Tips for sustaining new habits over the long term, including tracking progress, staying motivated, and dealing with setbacks.

Habits for Health and Well-being: A focus on key habits that promote physical, mental, and emotional health, such as regular exercise, healthy eating, adequate sleep, and stress management techniques.

Productivity and Time Management Habits: Examining habits that enhance efficiency and effectiveness in personal and professional endeavors.

By systematically addressing and refining your personal habits, you can dramatically transform your life. The journey of habit change is not always easy, but with persistence, the rewards can be profound. This section aims to guide you through the process of understanding your habits, making conscious decisions about which to cultivate or modify, and implementing strategies to ensure lasting change. Through this exploration, you'll discover that the power to create a more fulfilling life lies in the small choices you make every day.

Understanding The Role Of Habits

Understanding the role of habits in our lives is essential for personal growth and achieving our goals. Habits, the automatic behaviors we perform daily, significantly influence our health, productivity, relationships, and overall well-being. They form the backbone of our daily routines, saving us energy and time by reducing the number of decisions we need to make. This efficiency, however, is a double-edged sword, as it applies to both positive habits that benefit us and negative habits that hold us back.

Keystone Habits: A Foundation for Change

A powerful concept within the study of habits is that of "keystone habits." These are habits that, once established, can trigger a cascade of other beneficial behaviors, leading to widespread changes in our lives. Keystone habits have a multiplier effect, influencing various aspects of our lives and creating a structure that can foster further positive changes. They are foundational habits that can lead to the development of multiple good habits by creating momentum that spills over into other areas.

Characteristics of Keystone Habits

Create Far-Reaching Change: Keystone habits lead to a chain reaction of positive behavior changes, affecting various aspects of personal and professional life.

Offer Small Wins: They help in achieving small wins that boost self-confidence and motivation, encouraging further positive actions.

Establish a Structure: By fostering routines around which other habits can be organized, keystone habits help in creating a stable foundation for life improvements.

Foster a Culture of Success: When applied in organizational or group settings, keystone habits can influence the collective behavior, creating a culture of success and productivity.

Examples of Keystone Habits

Regular Exercise: Committing to regular physical activity can be a keystone habit that improves physical health, enhances mood, boosts energy levels, and can lead to better eating habits and improved sleep patterns.

Daily Planning: Taking time each day to plan tasks and set priorities can improve time management, reduce stress, and increase productivity, influencing work performance and personal satisfaction.

Mindful Eating: Adopting habits of mindful eating can lead to healthier food choices, better digestion, and can trigger a greater awareness of the body's needs, influencing overall health.

Gratitude Journaling: Regularly writing down things you're grateful for can enhance well-being, improve relationships, and foster a positive outlook on life, impacting emotional and mental health.

Developing Keystone Habits

To develop keystone habits, start by identifying areas of your life you wish to improve and consider habits that could have the most significant positive impact. Focus on small, manageable changes and be consistent in your efforts. It's also crucial to track your progress and celebrate small victories along the way, reinforcing the positive impact of your keystone habits.

Understanding and leveraging the power of keystone habits can be a game-changer in personal development. By focusing on key behaviors that set the stage for wider changes, you can streamline your efforts towards achieving your goals, enhancing your quality of life in the process.

Developing Healthy Habits

Developing healthy habits is a cornerstone of personal growth and well-being. By establishing routines that promote physical, mental, and emotional health, you can significantly improve your quality of life. To support the development and maintenance of these habits, tracking your progress is crucial. A habit-tracking template or utilizing digital tools can provide the structure and motivation needed to stick with your new routines. Here's a guide on how to develop healthy habits, including a simple habit-tracking template and recommendations for digital tools.

Developing Healthy Habits

Start Small: Choose one or two habits to focus on initially. Starting small makes it more likely you'll stick with the change.

Be Specific: Clearly define what your new habit will entail. For instance, instead of "exercise more," opt for "walk 30 minutes a day."

Anchor to Existing Routines: Link your new habit to an established part of your routine (e.g., meditate for 5 minutes after brushing your teeth in the morning).

Plan for Obstacles: Think about potential challenges and plan how you'll address them. This proactive approach can help you stay on track.

Reward Progress: Set up rewards for reaching milestones to maintain motivation.

Habit-Tracking Template

Creating a simple habit-tracking template can help you monitor your progress. Here's a basic format you can use on paper or in a digital spreadsheet:

Date	Habit 1 (e.g., Drink 8 Glasses of Water)	Habit 2 (e.g., 30 Min of Reading)	Notes
2024-01-01	Yes	Yes	Felt more relaxed at bedtime
2024-01-02	No	Yes	Forgot water bottle at home
2024-01-03	Yes	Yes	

Columns: Each column represents a different habit or the date and notes for additional context.

Rows: Each row corresponds to a day.

Marking: Mark "Yes" or "No" to indicate whether you completed the habit that day. Use the notes section for any relevant observations.

Digital Tools Recommendations

For those who prefer digital solutions, here are some highly-rated habit-tracking apps:

Habitica: Gamifies your habit formation by treating your goals like a role-playing game, complete with rewards and penalties to motivate you.

Loop Habit Tracker (Android): A simple, open-source habit tracker that allows you to create habits and track them with detailed graphs and statistics.

Streaks (iOS): Helps you track up to 12 habits at a time, displaying your current streak for each habit to motivate you to keep going.

HabitBull: Available on both iOS and Android, HabitBull offers detailed tracking, reminders, and motivational quotes to keep you focused on your goals.

Tally: A flexible tracking app that allows you to count and track anything. Its simplicity is perfect for those who want a straightforward, no-frills habit tracker.

Using a habit-tracking template or digital tool can significantly enhance your ability to develop and maintain healthy habits. By providing a visual representation of your progress, you're more likely to stay motivated and accountable, paving the way for lasting change.

Breaking Negative Habits

Breaking negative habits is a challenging yet rewarding process that requires understanding, strategy, and persistence. Negative habits, often formed over years, can be deeply ingrained, making them difficult to change. However, with the right approach, it's possible to replace them with healthier behaviors. Here are effective strategies for breaking negative habits and fostering positive change in your life.

1. Understand Your Habits

Identify the Habit: Clearly define the habit you want to change. Be specific about what the behavior entails and when it usually occurs.

Understand the Trigger: Every habit is triggered by a specific cue, such as a time of day, emotional state, or sequence of events. Identifying your triggers can help you anticipate and avoid them.

Recognize the Reward: Habits persist because they provide some form of reward, like stress relief or a sense of pleasure. Understanding what reward your habit provides can help you find healthier ways to achieve the same outcome.

2. Set Clear, Achievable Goals

Break down your goal of breaking the habit into smaller, manageable steps. Instead of aiming to eliminate a habit overnight, focus on gradually reducing your reliance on it.

3. Find a Substitute Behavior

For every habit you're trying to break, find a positive behavior to replace it. If stress triggers your negative habit, identify a healthier stress-reduction technique to use instead, like deep breathing or going for a walk.

4. Change Your Environment

Altering your environment can reduce exposure to triggers. If certain locations, people, or routines make your negative habit more likely, try to avoid them or change how you interact with them.

5. Use Reminders and Cues for Positive Habits

Place visual reminders around your environment to encourage positive habits and discourage negative ones. For example, if you're trying to drink more water instead of snacking, keep a water bottle at your desk.

6. Implement a Tracking System

Monitor your progress using a habit tracker. Recording your successes and setbacks can provide valuable insights into patterns and progress, boosting motivation.

7. Seek Support

Share your goal with friends, family, or a support group. They can offer encouragement, hold you accountable, and provide advice based on their experiences.

8. Reward Yourself

Set up a reward system for reaching milestones in breaking your habit. Choose rewards that reinforce your new, healthier behavior.

9. Practice Self-Compassion

Breaking habits is hard, and setbacks are normal. Treat yourself with kindness and understanding when you slip up, and view each setback as a learning opportunity rather than a failure.

10. Be Patient and Persistent

Habit change takes time. Be patient with yourself and persistent in your efforts. Remember that every effort you make brings you one step closer to your goal.

11. Consider Professional Help

Some habits, especially those related to substance use or deeply ingrained behaviors, may require professional assistance. Don't hesitate to seek help from a therapist or counselor.

By applying these strategies, you can navigate the process of breaking negative habits with more clarity and confidence. Changing habits is a journey, not a sprint, and each step forward is a victory worth celebrating.

Practice Exercises To Improve Personal Habits

Improving personal habits, whether forming new ones or modifying existing behaviors, involves understanding the mechanisms of habit formation and consistently applying strategies that facilitate change. Here are practice exercises designed to help you enhance your personal habits through focused habit formation and modification activities.

1. Identify and Understand Your Current Habits

Exercise: Make a comprehensive list of your daily habits, categorizing them as positive, negative, or neutral. For each habit, identify the cue (trigger), routine (behavior), and reward. Understanding this loop is crucial for modifying existing habits or creating new ones.

2. Set Clear, Specific Goals

Exercise: Transform vague aspirations into clear, actionable goals. Instead of "get in shape," opt for "exercise for 30 minutes at least 3 times a week." Use the SMART criteria to ensure your goals are Specific, Measurable, Achievable, Relevant, and Time-bound.

3. Implement the Replacement Technique

Exercise: Choose a negative habit you want to change. Identify the cue and reward associated with this habit and find a positive behavior that satisfies the same reward. For instance, if stress triggers snacking on junk food (for comfort), replace it with a short walk or meditation session to relieve stress.

4. Develop Mini Habits

Exercise: Break down your goal into the smallest possible action that moves you toward your desired habit, making it almost too easy not to do. If your goal is to read more, start with one page a night. Gradually increase the complexity as the habit becomes ingrained.

5. Use Habit Stacking

Exercise: Link a new habit to an established routine, creating a compound habit. For example, if you already have a habit of drinking coffee every morning, stack a new habit of writing a to-do list for the day with your coffee ritual.

6. Create a Supportive Environment

Exercise: Modify your environment to make good habits easier and bad habits harder. If you want to eat healthier, stock your fridge with healthy snacks and keep junk food out of the house. If you aim to reduce screen time before bed, charge your phone outside the bedroom.

7. Employ Visual Cues and Reminders

Exercise: Place visual cues in your environment to trigger positive habits. For example, leave your workout clothes and shoes next to your bed to encourage morning exercise. Use sticky notes, alarms, or habit-tracking apps as reminders for new habits.

8. Track Your Progress

Exercise: Create a habit tracker in a notebook or use a digital app. Record your daily progress with each habit you're working on. Tracking helps maintain motivation and provides insight into your progress and areas needing adjustment.

9. Reward Yourself for Milestones

Exercise: Set up a reward system for reaching milestones in your habit formation. Choose rewards that reinforce your new habit and don't contradict your goals. For instance, reward a week of completed workouts with a massage rather than a binge-eating session.

10. Reflect and Adjust

Exercise: Schedule regular intervals (weekly or monthly) to reflect on your habit format on progress. Assess what's working, what isn't, and why. Use th s reflection to make necessary adjustments to your strategies or goals.

By engaging in these exercises, you not only work towards forming new beneficial habits but also gain deeper insights into your behavior patterns. This process of continuous reflection and adjustment is key to developing lasting personal habits that align with your goals and enhance your overall well-being.

10. Learning And Personal Development

Lifelong Journeys of Growth

In the ever-evolving landscape of our lives, learning and personal development stand as pillars that support our journey towards fulfillment, success, and self-discovery. Far beyond the confines of traditional education, this continuous process of growth encompasses the acquisition of knowledge, skills, and experiences that shape our understanding of ourselves, others, and the world around us. It's about expanding our horizons, challenging our limitations, and striving towards our full potential.

This section is dedicated to exploring the vast terrain of learning and personal development, offering insights, strategies, and practical tools to foster a lifelong commitment to growth. Whether you're seeking to advance your career, enrich your personal life, or simply cultivate a deeper sense of curiosity, the path of learning and development is rich with opportunities for enhancement and transformation.

Key Areas Covered:

The Importance of Continuous Learning: An exploration of how lifelong learning benefits not only our professional lives but also our personal growth and well-being.

Setting Learning Goals: Guidance on identifying areas for development and setting specific, achievable learning objectives that align with your broader life goals.

Strategies for Effective Learning: Best practices and techniques for learning new skills and knowledge, including active learning, spaced repetition, and the application of learning to real-life situations.

Overcoming Obstacles to Learning: Identifying common barriers to learning and personal development, such as time constraints, fear of failure, and lack of motivation, and offering strategies to overcome these challenges.

Harnessing the Power of Habits for Learning: How to develop habits that support continuous learning and personal development, making growth a natural and integral part of your daily routine.

Leveraging Technology for Learning: An overview of digital tools and resources that can enhance the learning process, including online courses, podcasts, and mobile apps.

The Role of Reflection in Personal Development: Techniques for reflecting on your learning experiences, integrating new insights, and applying them to your personal and professional life.

Building a Personal Learning Network: Tips for cultivating a network of mentors, peers, and resources that can support and enrich your learning journey.

Mindsets for Success: Cultivating a growth mindset and other positive attitudes that foster resilience, openness to new experiences, and a willingness to learn from failure.

Integrating Learning into Everyday Life: Practical ideas for making learning an ongoing part of your life, from integrating educational activities into your routine to seeking out new experiences that challenge and inspire you.

Embarking on a path of learning and personal development is a commitment to yourself—to your growth, happiness, and fulfillment. This section aims to equip you with the knowledge, inspiration, and tools needed to embrace this journey, opening doors to endless possibilities and a richer, more rewarding life. Let's begin this adventure together, with curiosity as our guide and growth as our destination.

Importance Of Continuous Learning

Continuous learning and personal development are pivotal in today's rapidly changing world. They represent an investment in oneself that yields dividends across all aspects of life, from career advancement and personal fulfillment to improved relationships and overall well-being. The importance of this lifelong journey stems from its profound impact on adaptability and resilience, two qualities that are indispensable in navigating both personal and professional challenges.

Adaptability Through Continuous Learning

In an era marked by technological advancements, globalization, and shifting societal norms, the ability to adapt is crucial. Continuous learning fuels adaptability by:

Keeping Skills Relevant: As industries evolve, staying updated with the latest skills and knowledge ensures relevance and competitiveness in the job market.

Promoting Open-mindedness: Exposure to new ideas and diverse perspectives fosters an open mind, making it easier to adjust to new situations and embrace change.

Enhancing Problem-solving Abilities: Learning cultivates critical thinking and creativity, equipping individuals with the tools to tackle challenges innovatively.

Resilience Through Personal Development

Personal development plays a key role in building resilience, the capacity to recover quickly from difficulties. It contributes to resilience by:

Fostering Emotional Intelligence: Understanding and managing one's emotions, a core aspect of personal development, is vital for navigating stress and setbacks.

Building a Strong Self-concept: Engaging in personal development helps individuals understand their strengths and weaknesses, leading to a stronger sense of self and confidence in their abilities to overcome adversity.

Cultivating a Growth Mindset: Individuals committed to personal development often develop a growth mindset, seeing challenges as opportunities to learn and grow rather than insurmountable obstacles.

Practical Benefits of Personal Development

Career Advancement: Continuous learning can lead to new opportunities, promotions, and career transitions by showcasing a commitment to self-improvement and excellence.

Enhanced Life Satisfaction: Engaging in personal development activities has been linked to higher levels of life satisfaction and happiness.

Improved Relationships: Skills gained through personal development, such as communication and empathy, can lead to stronger, more meaningful relationships.

Strategies for Incorporating Personal Development

Set Clear Goals: Identify specific areas for growth and set achievable goals to guide your learning and development efforts.

Seek Feedback: Regular feedback from peers, mentors, or supervisors can provide valuable insights into areas for improvement.

Embrace Challenges: Step out of your comfort zone and embrace challenges as opportunities to learn and grow.

Leverage Resources: Take advantage of the myriad resources available, from online courses and workshops to books and podcasts.

Reflect Regularly: Take time to reflect on your experiences, what you've learned, and how you've grown. Reflection is a critical component of the learning process.

Continuous learning and personal development are not just activities to be pursued in one's spare time; they are essential strategies for thriving in today's dynamic environment. By fostering adaptability and resilience, individuals can navigate life's challenges with confidence and grace, turning obstacles into opportunities for growth.

Strategies For Continuous Learning And Growth

Continuous learning and growth are essential for personal and professional development in an ever-evolving world. Adopting strategies that foster a culture of lifelong learning can significantly enhance one's adaptability, resilience, and success. Among the myriad strategies available, mentorship and networking stand out for their unique roles in facilitating continuous learning and offering opportunities for growth. Here's how these elements contribute to a comprehensive strategy for lifelong development:

The Role of Mentorship

1. Guidance and Insight: Mentors provide valuable guidance, sharing their experiences, mistakes, and successes. This insight can help mentees navigate their own paths more effectively, avoiding common pitfalls and leveraging opportunities more fully.

2. Accountability and Encouragement: Having a mentor can increase your accountability, keeping you focused on your learning goals. Mentors also offer encouragement and support, which is crucial during challenging times or when facing setbacks.

3. Skill Development: Mentors can identify areas for improvement and offer targeted advice to develop specific skills. Whether it's improving leadership abilities, technical skills, or soft skills, mentors can provide personalized feedback and resources.

4. Expanding Perspectives: Exposure to a mentor's knowledge and experiences can broaden your perspective, challenging you to think in new ways and consider alternative approaches to problems.

Strategies for Effective Mentorship

Seek Diverse Mentors: Look for mentors who can offer diverse perspectives and experiences. Diversity in mentorship can inspire innovative thinking and creativity.

Be Proactive in the Relationship: Take the initiative to set goals for the mentorship, ask questions, and seek feedback. The more you put into the relationship, the more you'll get out of it.

Apply What You Learn: Demonstrate your commitment to growth by applying your mentor's advice and sharing your progress with them.

The Importance of Networking

1. Access to New Ideas and Knowledge: Networking introduces you to a wide range of people, each with unique knowledge and experiences. Engaging with your network can expose you to new ideas, trends, and best practices.

2. Opportunities for Collaboration: Networking can lead to opportunities for collaboration, allowing you to work with others on projects or initiatives that facilitate mutual growth.

3. Career Opportunities: A robust network can open doors to job opportunities, partnerships, and other career advancements that you might not have access to otherwise.

4. Support System: A network can serve as a support system, offering advice, feedback, and encouragement. Networking groups, whether professional associations or informal gatherings, can be invaluable sources of motivation and inspiration.

Strategies for Effective Networking

Be Genuine: Approach networking with a genuine interest in others. Seek to build relationships rather than merely extracting value from contacts.

Offer Value: Think about how you can offer value to your network, whether through sharing information, providing support, or connecting people with similar interests.

Stay Engaged: Regularly engage with your network through social media, attending events, or scheduling catch-ups. Consistency keeps relationships strong and ensures you remain fresh in people's minds.

Leverage Social Media: Platforms like LinkedIn, Twitter, and industry-specific forums can be powerful tools for expanding your network and engaging with thought leaders in your field.

Mentorship and networking are powerful strategies for continuous learning and growth, offering a wealth of resources, support, and opportunities. By actively seeking out mentors and cultivating a robust professional network, you can accelerate your personal and professional development, staying adaptable and forward-thinking in an ever-changing world.

Reading, Attending Courses, And Pursuing Experiences

Reading, attending courses, and pursuing diverse experiences are pivotal strategies for enriching one's knowledge base, skills, and understanding of the world. These activities not only broaden perspectives but also inspire innovation and creativity. Here's a curated resource list to facilitate further exploration in continuous learning and personal development:

Reading Resources

"Atomic Habits" by James Clear: Offers practical strategies for forming good habits, breaking bad ones, and mastering the tiny behaviors that lead to remarkable results.

"Mindset: The New Psychology of Success" by Carol S. Dweck: Explores the concept of "mindset" and how an individual's view of themselves can profoundly affect all areas of their life.

"The 7 Habits of Highly Effective People" by Stephen R. Covey: A classic book on personal effectiveness and leadership that has inspired millions to transform their thinking and actions.

"How to Win Friends and Influence People" by Dale Carnegie: Teaches essential interpersonal skills and strategies for navigating relationships successfully.

"Deep Work: Rules for Focused Success in a Distracted World" by Cal Newport: Discusses the benefits of deep work and provides strategies for cultivating focus and productivity.

Online Course Platforms

Coursera: Offers courses from universities and colleges around the world on a wide range of topics, from psychology and personal development to technical skills.

Udemy: Features a vast selection of courses on professional and personal development topics, including programming, design, photography, and business skills.

edX: Provides access to courses from institutions such as Harvard, MIT, and others, covering subjects like computer science, languages, and business management.

Skillshare: Focuses on creative skills, offering courses in areas like illustration, writing, music production, and graphic design.

LinkedIn Learning: Offers courses tailored towards professional development, including leadership, project management, and digital marketing.

Experiential Learning Opportunities

Volunteering: Organizations like VolunteerMatch and local community centers can connect you with volunteering opportunities that match your interests and skills, offering hands-on experience and the chance to make a difference.

Internships and Apprenticeships: Platforms like Internships.com and local trade organizations can help find opportunities to gain practical experience in your field of interest.

Travel: Engaging in cultural exchange programs or simply traveling with an open mind can provide invaluable life lessons and broaden your worldview.

Hobbies and Clubs: Joining clubs or groups related to your interests (e.g., photography, hiking, book clubs) can expand your knowledge and skills in a social setting.

Public Lectures and Workshops: Many universities, libraries, and community centers host free or low-cost public lectures and workshops on a variety of topics.

This resource list is a starting point for anyone looking to expand their horizons through reading, courses, and experiential learning. By engaging with these resources, you can continue to grow, challenge yourself, and enrich your personal and professional life.

Practice Exercises To Improve Personal Development Skills

Personal development is a continuous journey that involves learning new skills, enhancing existing ones, and reflecting on your growth and experiences. To support this journey, practice exercises that focus on planning and reflection can be incredibly beneficial. Below are exercises designed to improve personal development skills, including the creation of a learning plan template and the incorporation of reflective practices.

1. Create a Personalized Learning Plan

Objective: To identify areas for growth and outline specific steps to achieve personal development goals.

Assessment: Begin by assessing your current skills and knowledge. Identify areas where you wish to improve or learn new things.

Goal Setting: Use the SMART criteria to set specific, measurable, achievable, relevant, and time-bound goals related to your personal development.

Action Plan: For each goal, list the resources you'll use (books, courses, workshops), the timeline for achieving this goal, and the indicators of success.

Template:

Goal: [Your specific goal]

Resources Needed: [List of resources]

Timeline: [Start date – Completion date]

Success Indicators: [How you'll know the goal has been achieved]

Reflection Points: [Scheduled times to reflect on progress]

Follow-Up: Regularly review and adjust your learning plan based on your progress and any new goals that arise.

2. Engage in Reflective Practice

Objective: To integrate reflection into your personal development process, enhancing learning and growth.

Daily Reflection: At the end of each day, spend 5-10 minutes reflecting on what you learned, challenges you faced, and how you dealt with them. Consider what worked well and what could be improved.

Journaling: Keep a reflective journal to document your thoughts, feelings, and insights related to your personal development journey. Use it to explore successes, setbacks, and areas for growth.

Questions for Reflection:

What did I learn today/this week/this month?
How did I apply what I learned in a practical situation?
What challenges did I encounter, and how did I overcome them?
How have I grown in my personal or professional life as a result of these experiences?
What new goals or areas of improvement have I identified?

Follow-Up: Use insights gained from reflective practice to adjust your learning plan and set new development goals.

3. Seek Feedback

Objective: To obtain external perspectives on your growth and areas for further development.

Identify individuals whose opinions you value (mentors, colleagues, friends).

Ask for specific feedback on areas you're working to improve. Request both strengths and areas for growth.

Reflect on the feedback received and how it aligns with your self-assessment.

Follow-Up: Incorporate this feedback into your learning plan, adjusting goals and strategies as needed.

4. Set Up a Peer Learning Group

Objective: To learn collaboratively with others, sharing knowledge, skills, and experiences.

Form a group with peers interested in personal and professional development.

Meet regularly to discuss your goals, progress, and challenges.

Share resources, insights, and feedback to support each other's growth.

Follow-Up: Leverage the group for accountability, motivation, and deeper learning.

These practice exercises offer a structured approach to personal development, encouraging continuous learning, reflection, and adaptation. By actively engaging in these exercises, you can foster a growth mindset, achieve your personal development goals, and navigate your journey of lifelong learning with purpose and insight.

Conclusion

Conclusion: Embracing the Journey of Personal Growth

As we reach the conclusion of our exploration into personal growth and development, it's clear that the journey is both complex and rewarding. Throughout this guide, we've delved into various facets of self-improvement, from understanding the power of mindset and emotional intelligence to mastering effective communication, managing time, setting meaningful goals, and beyond. Each section has offered insights and practical exercises designed to foster a deeper understanding of oneself and to cultivate the skills necessary for thriving in today's dynamic world.

The essence of personal development lies not in a destination but in the ongoing journey of discovery, learning, and growth. It's about continuously evolving, facing challenges with resilience, and seeking out opportunities for expansion in all areas of life. As we conclude, it's important to reflect on the key takeaways and to consider how they can be integrated into daily life to foster ongoing growth.

Key Takeaways:

Mindset and Attitude: Cultivating a growth mindset and positive attitude is foundational to overcoming obstacles and achieving personal growth.

Self-Awareness and Emotional Intelligence: Understanding oneself and managing emotions effectively are crucial for personal and professional success.

Communication and Relationships: Effective communication skills enhance relationships, fostering deeper connections and understanding.

Time Management and Goal Setting: Managing time efficiently and setting clear goals are essential for productivity and achieving one's aspirations.

Continuous Learning: Lifelong learning and adaptability are keys to navigating the ever-changing landscape of life and career.

Resilience and Coping: Developing resilience and effective coping strategies enables individuals to face challenges with strength and grace.

As you move forward, remember that personal development is a personal journey, unique to each individual. It requires patience, persistence, and a willingness to explore and embrace change. The strategies and exercises provided in this guide are starting points—tools to be adapted and built upon as you continue on your path of growth.

In closing, we encourage you to keep an open mind, to remain curious, and to approach each day as an opportunity to learn something new about yourself and the world around you. Personal growth is an endless horizon, rich with possibilities and opportunities for enrichment. Embrace the journey with enthusiasm and optimism, and let your quest for development be guided by a spirit of discovery and a heart full of courage. Here's to your continued growth and success on this lifelong journey of personal development.

Recap Of The Main Points Covered In The Book

This book has taken you on a comprehensive journey through the multifaceted landscape of personal growth and development, offering insights, strategies, and practical exercises designed to enhance various aspects of your life. As we recap the main points covered, let's highlight the key insights and strategies that have emerged from each section, solidifying the foundation for your ongoing journey of self-improvement.

1. Introduction to Personal Growth and Development

Emphasized the importance of personal growth in today's fast-paced world and introduced the broad range of topics covered in the book.

2. Mindset and Attitude

Highlighted the transformative power of a positive mindset and growth attitude in overcoming challenges and achieving goals.

3. Self-Awareness

Discussed the crucial role of self-awareness in understanding one's strengths, weaknesses, values, and beliefs to foster personal and professional growth.

4. Emotional Intelligence

Explored the significance of emotional intelligence in managing emotions, enhancing relationships, and navigating social complexities.

5. Communication Skills

Addressed the importance of effective communication in improving interpersonal relationships and achieving success in various aspects of life.

6. Time Management

Offered strategies for managing time efficiently, prioritizing tasks, and overcoming procrastination to enhance productivity and achieve a balanced life.

7. Goal Setting

Detailed the process of setting meaningful, achievable goals using the SMART criteria and the importance of adaptability and persistence in goal attainment.

8. Mindfulness

Introduced mindfulness as a powerful practice for enhancing presence, reducing stress, and improving overall well-being.

9. Stress Management

Provided techniques and strategies for managing stress, building resilience, and maintaining mental and emotional health.

10. Personal Habits

Discussed the impact of personal habits on life and offered guidance on forming positive habits and breaking negative ones.

11. Learning and Personal Development

Emphasized the value of continuous learning and personal development in adapting to change, pursuing passions, and achieving lifelong goals.

Conclusion

I enjoy Encourage readers to embrace personal growth as a continuous, lifelong journey, highlighting the importance of curiosity, open-mindedness, and resilience.

Throughout this book, the recurring theme has been the power of intentional action and reflection in driving personal growth. By applying the strategies and exercises provided, you can build a solid foundation for continuous improvement, leading to a more fulfilling, balanced, and successful life.

As you move forward, remember that personal growth is not a destination but a journey. It requires commitment, patience, and the courage to step out of your comfort zone. With the insights and tools gained from this book, you are well-equipped to navigate the path of personal development, turning challenges into opportunities for growth and transformation. Keep exploring, learning, and growing, and let your journey of personal development be a rewarding adventure that unfolds throughout your life.

Final Thoughts On Personal Growth And Development

As we conclude this exploration into the realms of personal growth and development, it's important to recognize that the journey toward self-improvement is both infinite and deeply personal. The insights and strategies shared in this book are designed to serve as a compass, guiding you through the varied landscapes of your own growth journey. Remember, personal development is not a race, nor is it a competition. It is a lifelong commitment to becoming the best version of yourself, one step at a time.

The path to personal growth is paved with challenges, successes, setbacks, and discoveries. Each experience, whether perceived as positive or negative, carries valuable lessons that contribute to your development. Embrace these experiences with openness and curiosity, for they are the true catalysts of growth.

Call to Action

Now, as you stand at the threshold of your next chapter, it's time to take the insights from this book and turn them into action. Here's a call to action to propel you forward:

Reflect on Your Journey: Take a moment to reflect on your current state of personal growth. Where are you now, and where do you want to be? Consider what aspects of your life you're most eager to develop or transform.

Set Concrete Goals: Armed with your reflections, set concrete, achievable goals for your personal growth. Use the SMART criteria to ensure your goals are well-defined and attainable.

Create a Plan: Develop a plan of action that outlines the steps you'll take to achieve your goals. Include timelines, resources needed, and how you'll measure your progress.

Commit to Continuous Learning: Make a commitment to lifelong learning. Seek out books, courses, seminars, and experiences that will expand your knowledge and skills.

Build a Support Network: Surround yourself with a network of supporters, mentors, and peers who encourage your growth. Share your goals with them and ask for accountability and support.

Embrace Challenges: View challenges as opportunities for growth. When faced with obstacles, remind yourself of your ability to learn and adapt.

Practice Self-Compassion: Be kind to yourself as you embark on this journey. Celebrate your successes, learn from your setbacks, and treat yourself with compassion and understanding.

Reflect and Adjust: Regularly reflect on your progress and experiences. Be willing to adjust your goals and strategies as you learn and grow.

Take Action: Start today. Choose one small action you can take right now that will move you closer to your goals. Then, keep the momentum going by taking consistent, purposeful steps each day.

Your journey of personal growth and development is uniquely yours, filled with limitless potential and endless opportunities for learning and transformation. Embrace it with enthusiasm, courage, and an open heart. Remember, the most significant investment you can make is in yourself. Here's to your continued growth, discovery, and success on this extraordinary journey.

Encouragement To Continue The Journey

Embarking on the journey of self-discovery and growth is one of the most rewarding adventures you can undertake. It's a path that

leads to deeper self-awareness, fulfillment, and the realization of your fullest potential. As you continue to navigate this journey, remember that the pursuit of personal growth is ongoing—a process that flourishes with curiosity, commitment, and the courage to face challenges head-on.

Encouragement for Your Journey

Let each step on this path be guided by a deep sense of curiosity about yourself and the world around you. Embrace the unknown with an open heart and mind, ready to learn from every experience. Celebrate your victories, no matter how small, and view setbacks as valuable lessons that pave the way for growth. Most importantly, be patient and compassionate with yourself. Growth takes time, and every effort you make is a step forward in your journey.

Resources for Continued Learning and Development

To support you on your path, here's a list of resources that can offer guidance, inspiration, and practical tools for continued learning and development:

Books

"The Power of Now" by Eckhart Tolle: A guide to spiritual enlightenment and living in the present.

"Daring Greatly" by Brené Brown: Explores the importance of vulnerability in creating strong connections and living a full life.

"Atomic Habits" by James Clear: Offers strategies for forming good habits, breaking bad ones, and mastering the tiny behaviors that lead to remarkable results.

Online Learning Platforms

Coursera and **edX**: Offer courses from universities around the world on a wide range of topics.

Skillshare: Focuses on creative courses, such as photography, writing, and design.

MasterClass: Provides classes taught by world-renowned experts and celebrities in various fields.

Podcasts

"The Tim Ferriss Show": Features interviews with high achievers to uncover their routines and habits.

"Oprah's SuperSoul Conversations": Offers insights into personal growth and spirituality from thought leaders and best-selling authors.

Apps for Mindfulness and Habit Building

Headspace: Provides guided meditations for stress reduction and improved sleep.

Habitica: Gamifies your personal and professional goals to make habit formation fun.

Professional and Peer Networks

Meetup: Find local groups and events focused on personal development and specific interests.

LinkedIn Learning: Offers professional development courses with a focus on business, technology, and creative skills.

Journals and Planners

The Five Minute Journal: Designed for gratitude practice and focusing on the positive aspects of your life.

BestSelf Co. Self Journal: Helps with goal setting, productivity, and time management.

As you utilize these resources, remember that the journey of personal growth is uniquely yours. There's no one-size-fits-all approach, so feel free to explore different resources and methods to find what resonates with you. Stay committed to your path of self-discovery and growth, and know that every effort you make enriches your journey. Here's to your continued exploration, learning, and development, with the world as your classroom and life as your most profound teacher.

Manufactured by Amazon.ca
Acheson, AB